1 I am 'G'

Look at the letters given below. What is the difference between the two letters?

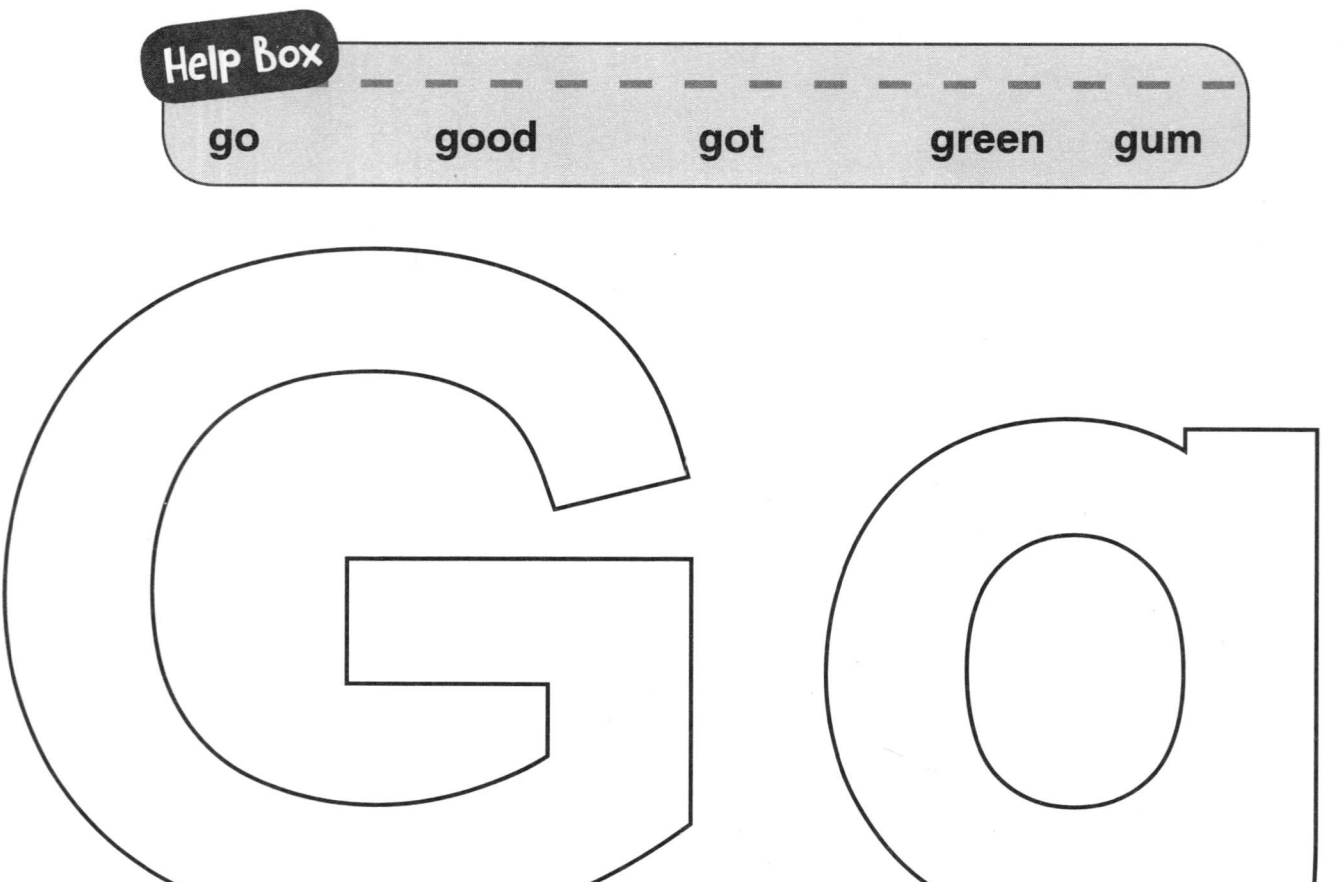

Help Box: go   good   got   green   gum

Now write the words given in the Help Box using capital 'G'.

_____   _____   _____

_____   _____

Date: _____   Teacher's Signature: _____

2   I Am an Igloo

Look at the figure given below. An igloo is hidden in the given figure. Colour capital letter 'I' and small letter 'i' with two different colours to find the picture.

Hint:

Igloo is white in colour and it looks like a tortoise. You can get a parent or an elder sibling to help you for this one.

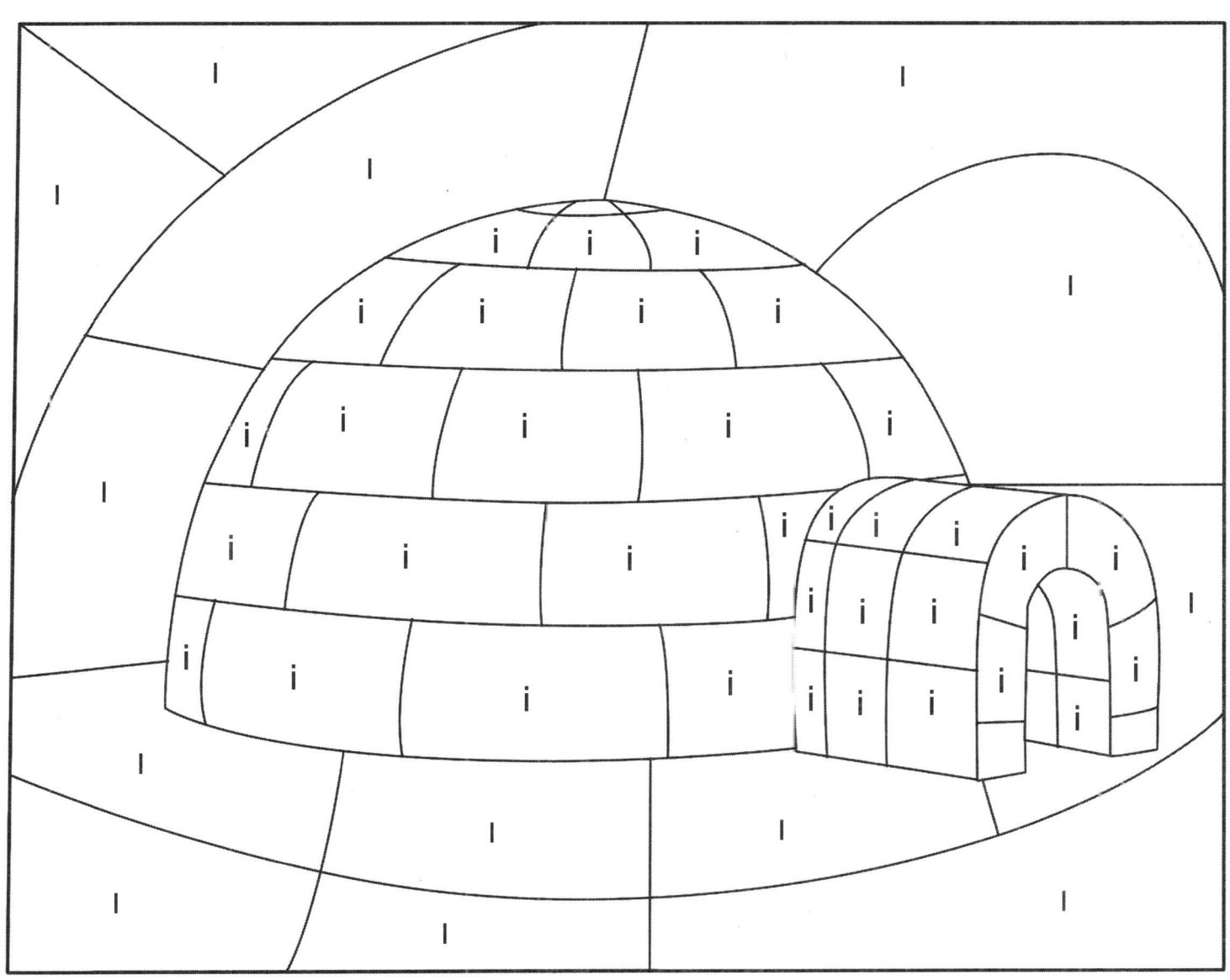

Date: _____   Teacher's Signature: _____

3 Missing Alphabet

Fill the missing alphabets and complete the alphabet grid.

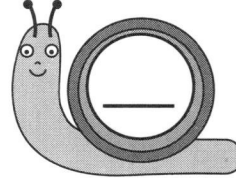  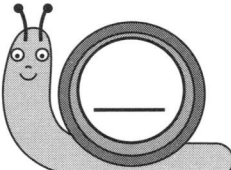 

 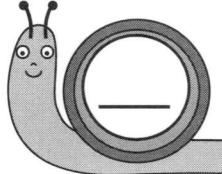   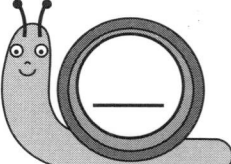

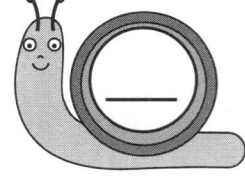   

 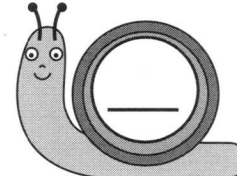 

Date: _____   Teacher's Signature: _____

4 'N' Route

Find the path from N to n by following the path of capital 'N' and small 'n'.

b	C	d	e	F	G	h	i	J	k	L	M	x	**N**	o
v	U	t	S	r	Q	N	n	N	n	N	n	N	n	P
W	N	n	N	n	x	n	Y	z	B	c	D	e	F	G
L	n	K	J	N	i	N	n	N	n	N	n	N	n	h
m	N	n	O	n	P	q	R	s	T	u	V	w	N	x
C	n	B	z	N	n	N	n	N	n	N	n	N	n	Y
d	N	e	F	g	H	i	J	k	L	m	Y	o	p	q
X	n	N	n	N	w	V	u	T	s	N	n	N	n	R
y	Z	b	C	n	D	n	N	n	N	n	E	f	N	G
S	r	Q	p	N	o	N	z	M	l	K	j	l	n	H
t	N	n	N	n	U	n	V	w	X	y	Z	b	N	c
J	n	l	h	G	f	N	e	N	n	N	n	N	n	D
k	N	n	N	n	N	n	L	n	M	c	O	p	Q	r
g	F	e	D	c	B	z	y	N	x	W	v	U	t	S
H	i	J	k	L	m	F	o	**n**	P	q	R	S	T	U

Date: _____   Teacher's Signature: _____

5

5   Play with Sound 'E'

Read the words given below and colour the pictures that have an 'E' sound.

I Am 'T'

Find out what picture is hidden inside. Colour capital letter 'T' with brown colour. Colour small letter 't' with blue colour.

Hint: It's a vehicle.

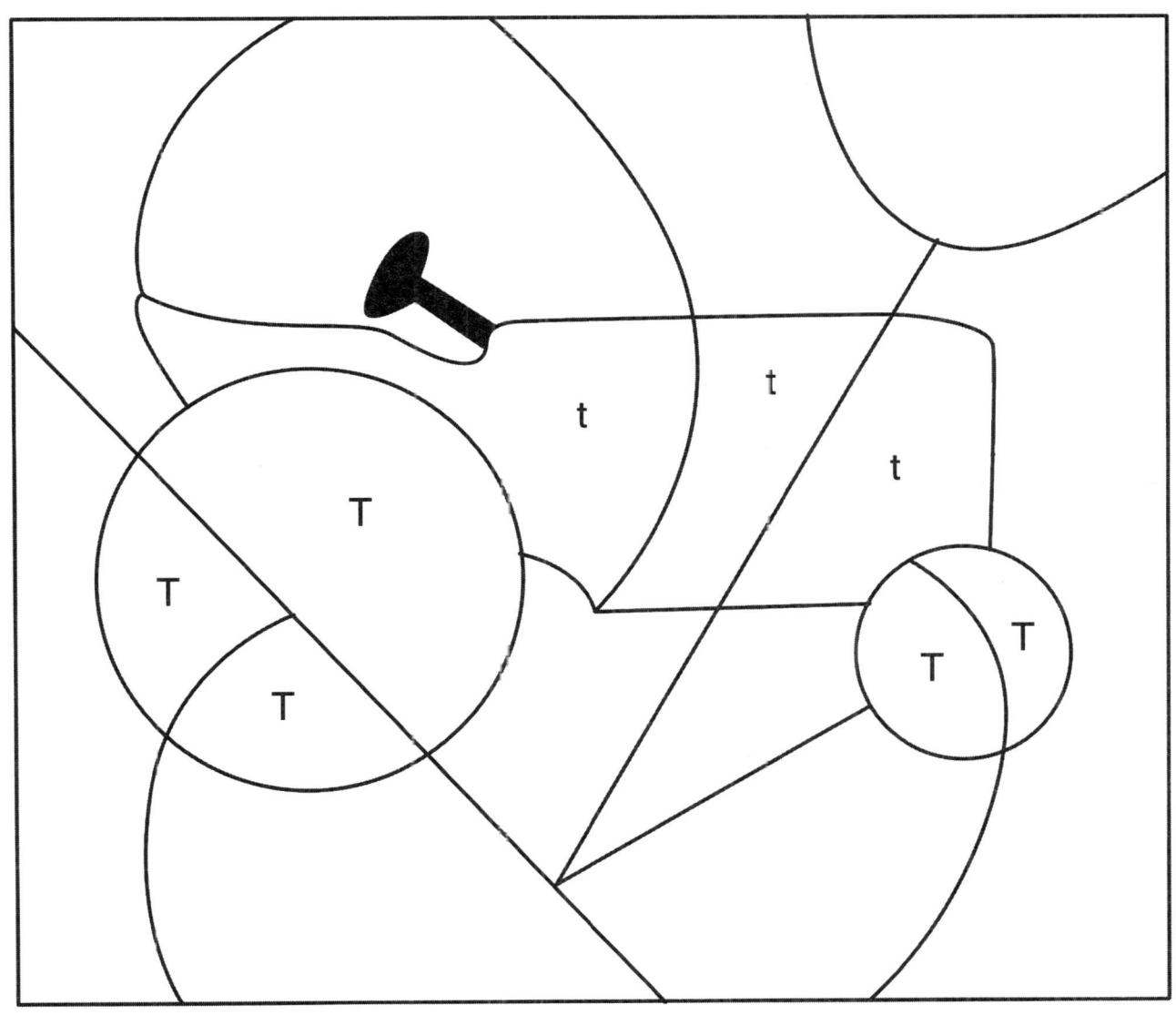

I am a _____.

Date: _____   Teacher's Signature: _____

1 All Capital

Look at the picture given below. What is it? Write its name in capital letters. Also, write all the other words in the Help Box using capital letters.

_____

Help Box

the   ten   to   this   that

_____   _____   _____

_____   _____

Date: _____   Teacher's Signature: _____

8 — 'C' in a Plant

Find out what picture is hidden. Colour capital 'C' with green colour. Colour small 'c' with yellow colour.

Hint: I am a spiky plant. If you need, you can ask a parent or an elder to help you identify this plant.

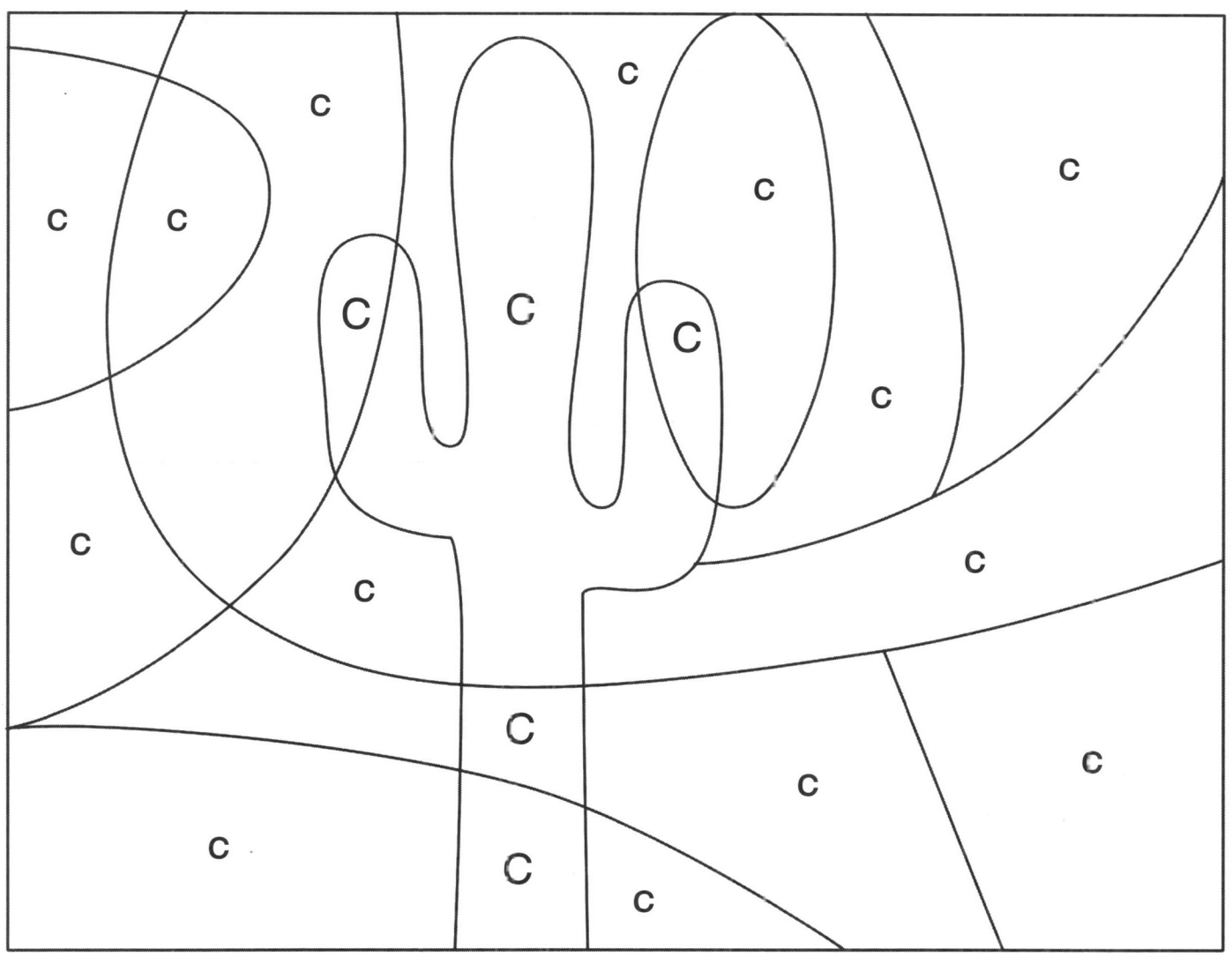

I am a _____ .

Date: _____   Teacher's Signature: _____

9 Enjoy Boating

The boy in the picture is happily boating on a lake. Use the words given in the Help Box to give this picture a suitable caption like the one given below.

Help Box

| Jack | loves | lake | boating | with |
| water | friends | like | fish | frog |

Example: Jack Loves Boating

Teacher's Signature: _____

10   I Am Your Hat

A hat is hidden in the given figure. Use two different colours to colour capital 'H' and small 'h'.

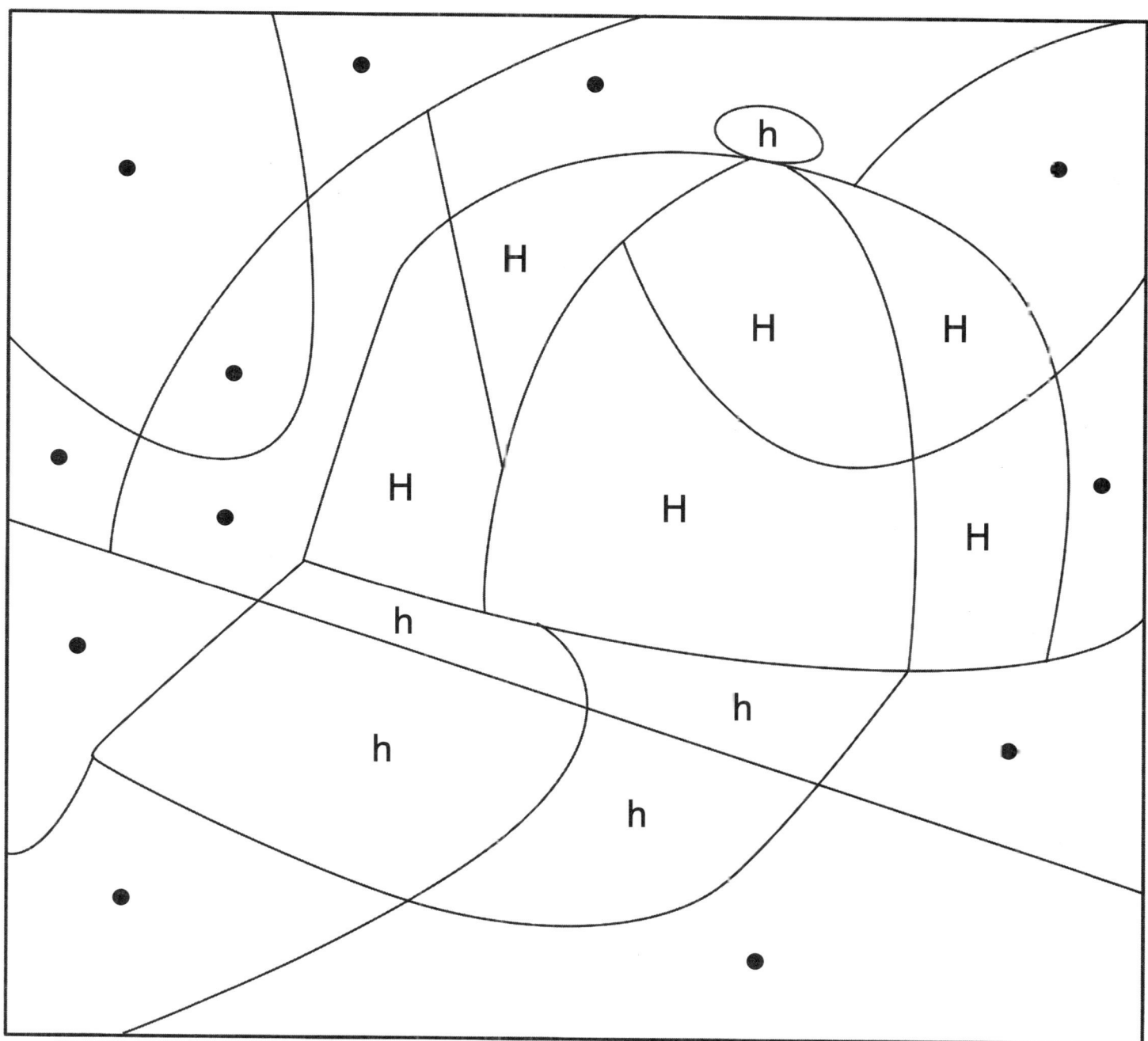

11 It's Playtime

Look at the picture given below. Arrange the words given in the Word Bank to form a meaningful sentence related to the picture and colour it.

Word Bank

golf   A   playing   under the sun   is   dinosaur

_____

_____

_____

_____

_____

Date: _____   Teacher's Signature: _____

12 Nature Match

Match the pictures with the correct phrase.

Sun with clouds

Moon with clouds

Hill

River Valley

13 Rhyming Words

Read this rhyme carefully. Now find four rhyming words in it and write them in the given space.

Down behind the dustbin

Down behind the dustbin.

I met a dog called Ted.

"Leave me alone," he says,

"I'm just going to bed."

Down behind the dustbin.

I met a dog called Roger.

"Do you own this bin?" I said.

"No. I am only a lodger," he said.

Rhyming words are:

Date: _____   Teacher's Signature: _____

14 Travelling with Wheels

Observe the pictures carefully and circle the pictures showing modes of transport that use wheels.

What type of 'E' sound does the word 'wheel' have? Tick (✓) the correct answer.

A long 'E' sound   _____

A short 'E' sound   _____

Date: _____   Teacher's Signature: _____

15 How's the Weather Today?

Go out of the house and observe the weather. Tick (✓) the smiley and show how you feel about the weather?

 Happy

 It is ok

 Angry

 Sad

Date: _____ Teacher's Signature: _____

I Like To...

**Which of these activities have you done the most? Tick (✓) it.
Which of these activities would you love to do? Colour it.**

17 Describe in One Word

Observe the images related to weather. Pick and write a suitable word from the bracket that describes it.

_____ **(warm/cotton)**

_____ **(chilly/hot)**

_____ **(woollen/thin)**

_____ **(tangy/bitter)**

Date: _____ Teacher's Signature: _____

18 We Must, We Must Not

What is right? Tick (✓) in the correct column.

Things	We must	We must not
Eat lots of		
Eat		
Drink		
Brush my		

Date: _____

Teacher's Signature: _____

19 Grow Baby Grow

See the pictures given below. First trace the word and then fill in the blanks with the same word. What did you learn from it?

Babies _____ so fast.

Date: _____ Teacher's Signature: _____

20   I Know It All!

Tick (✓) the correct answers.

a. I brush my

    i. once a week   ii. twice a day

b. We feel the softness of  by touching its

    i. skin   ii. eye

C. We smell the  using our

    i. nose   ii. ears

d. When we  , we must say

    i. good night   ii. sorry

Date: _____   Teacher's Signature: _____

21 We Rhyme

Read the following rhyme carefully and identify four rhyming words in it.

Hey, diddle, diddle,

The cat and the fiddle

The cow jumped over the moon;

The little dog laughed

to see such sport,

And the dish ran away with the spoon.

Rhyming words are:

22 Complete the Table

Look at the pictures and complete the table with Yes or No.

Object	Do I need food and water?	Do I need air?	Do I grow?	Do I reproduce?	Am I living?
(chick hatching)					
(sun and clouds)					
(fire)					
(mountain and river)					
(ladybug)					

Date: _____   Teacher's Signature: _____

23 How Do I Look?

Look at the pictures given below. Choose the right slogan for each picture and write it in the space near them.

Slogan 1: Fatty Me

Slogan 2: Stronger Me

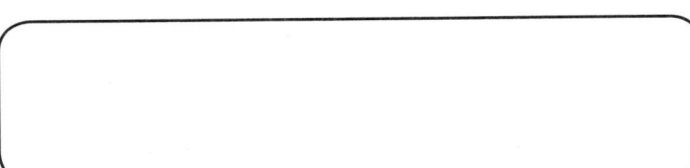

Date: _____   Teacher's Signature: _____

24 A Note for Mom and Dad

Read the note written below. Now look at the two cards here. Copy the note below the card best suited for the note.

Thank You Mummy and Papa
I love you
Yours

(_____)

Date: _____   Teacher's Signature: _____

25 Indian Flag

Match the flags with their countries.

USA

United Kingdom

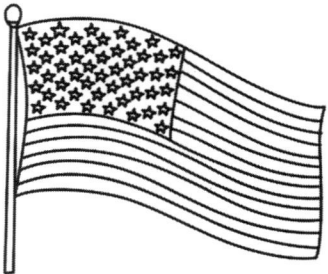

India

China

Date: _____   Teacher's Signature: _____

26 Words With 'Wh'

How many words start with 'Wh' in the box given below? Circle them and write the number of words.

We	What
White	Who
Why	With

The number of 'Wh' words: _____

Date: _____   Teacher's Signature: _____

27 My Fruit Plate

Look at the picture given below. Choose your favourite fruits and draw them to make your own plate of fruits.

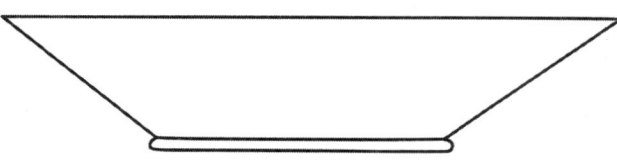

Date: _____

Teacher's Signature: _____

28   I Don't Belong Here

Circle the thing in each row that does not belong to the group.

1.

2.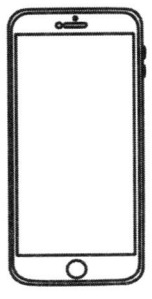

3.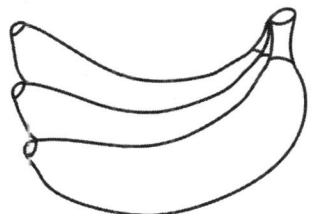

4.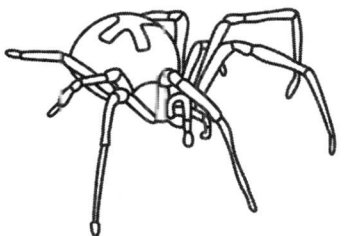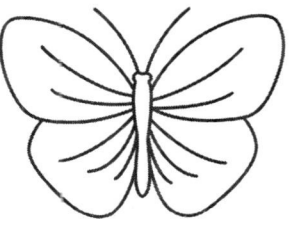

Date: _____   Teacher's Signature: _____

29 Let's Compare

Read the sentence with each set of pictures and circle the correct answer. The first one has been done for you.

I am smaller.

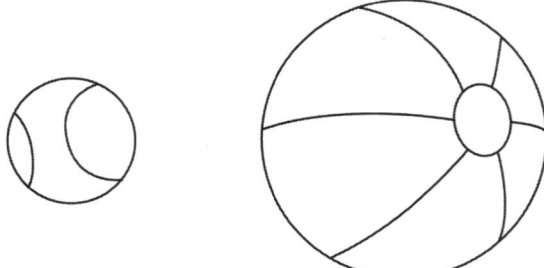

I am bigger.

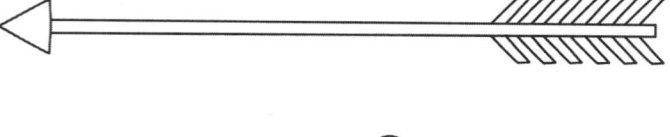

I am stronger.

I am smaller.

I am broader.

I am lighter.

31   I Love Vegetables

Look at the picture given below. Choose your favourite vegetables, draw and colour them to make your own plate of vegetables.

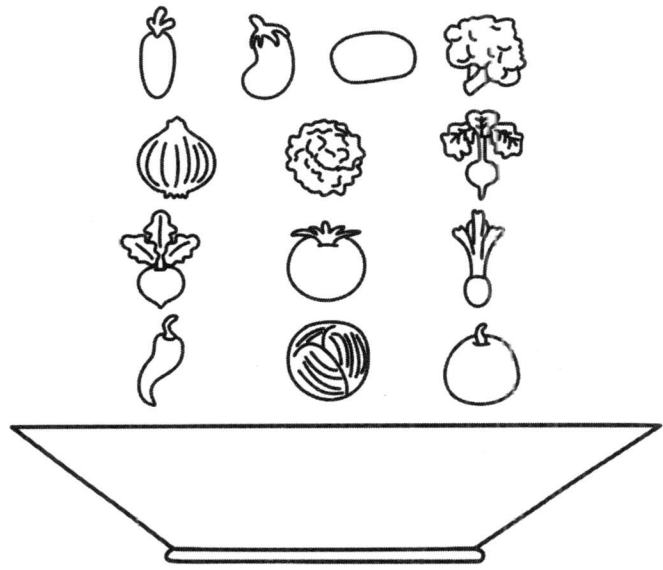

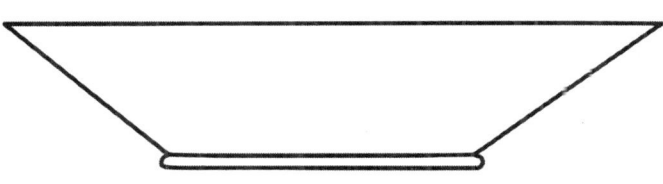

30 Missing Letter

Choose the common alphabet from Group B that will complete the word in Group A.

A

___ e s t

B

no   new   nice

nine   now   not

Date: _____   Teacher's Signature: _____

33 I Appear at Night

Look at the picture given below. Choose the alphabet that is common among the words in the Help Box and that will help you complete the word.

Help Box

MAP   MAT   MUG   MY   ME

___ o o n

32 It's Not a Cap

Choose the correct alphabet from the Help Box to complete the word.

Help Box

B	G	H	T	R	K	C

__ A T

Date: ____________   Teacher's Signature: ____________

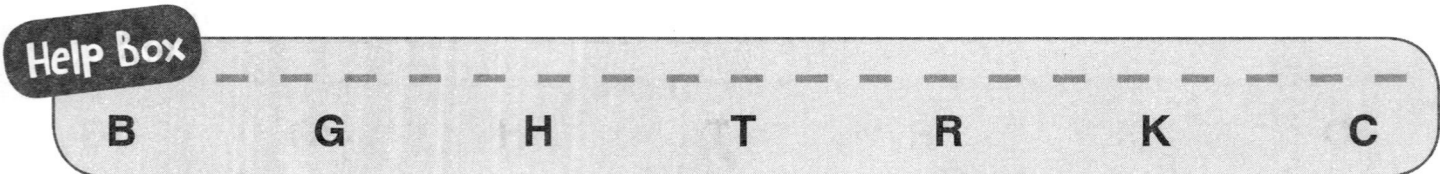

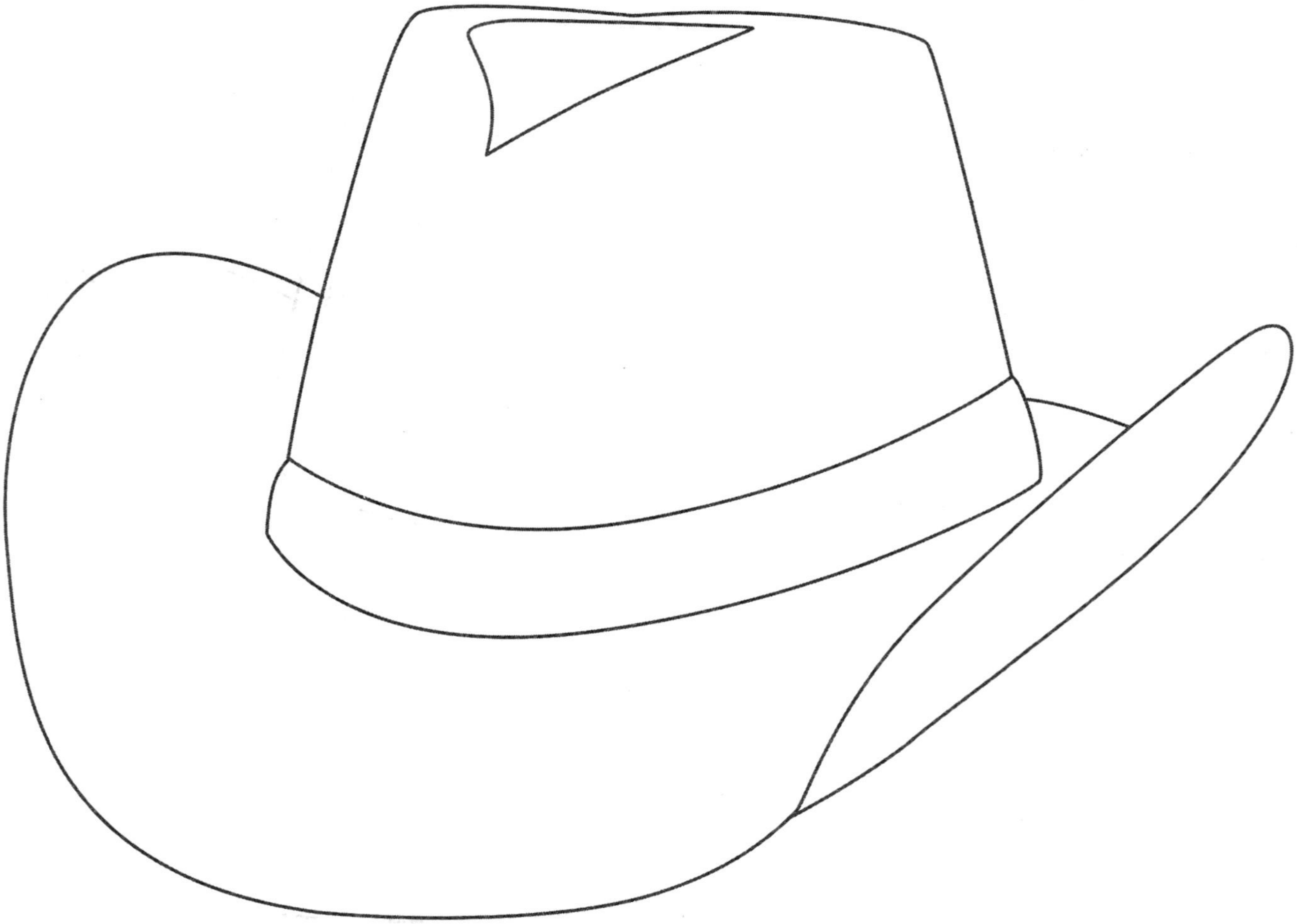

I Am an Insect

Look at the picture given below. Its name rhymes with the words given in the Help Box. Read them aloud and fill in the missing letter.

Help Box

MUG   JUG   RUG

B ___ G

35   I Always Smile

Search letters from the word grid that describes the smiley. Follow the word search directions carefully to find the correct word.

DIRECTIONS

1st letter from 1st line.

5th letter from 3rd line.

3rd letter from 1st line.

2nd letter from 4th line.

1st letter from 2nd line.

I Am a Colour

How many names of colours can you find in the box that starts with the letter 'B'? Circle and colour them with that colour.

BLACK	BROWN
BLUE	BUT
CAME	CAN

Date: _____   Teacher's Signature: _____

The 'S' Numbers

How many numbers can you find in the following words that start with letter 'S'? Write only those numbers in numericals.

SEVEN	SHE
SIX	SMALL
TEN	SOON

_____   _____

Trace Lines

Trace the lines and identify the animal.

Hint: The name of the animal is there in the Help Box.

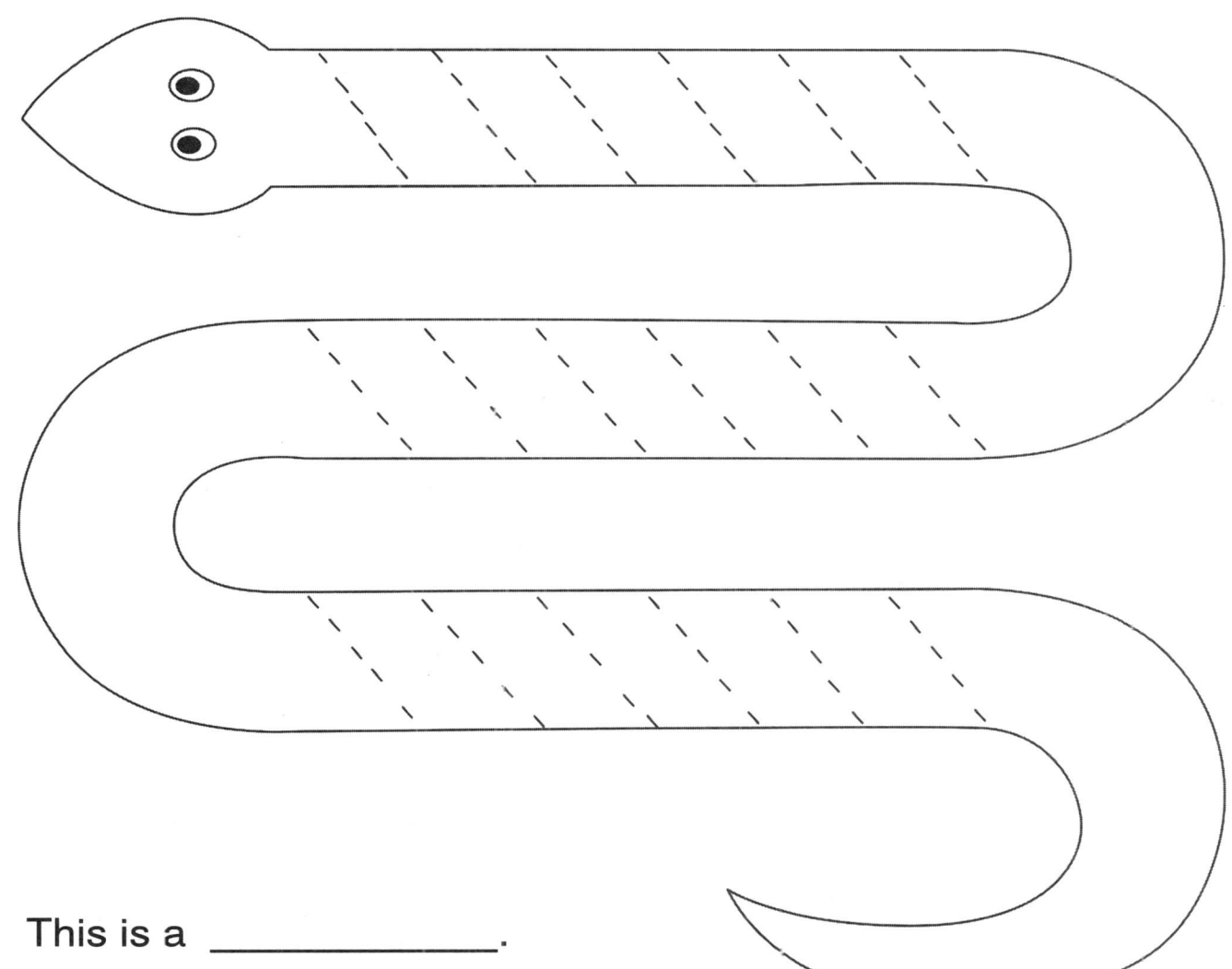

This is a _____.

Help Box

Tortoise   Sheep   Snake   Worm

Date: _____

39 The ABCD Sudoku

Fill each blank square with the correct letter. The letters A, B, C and D must appear only once in each row and column.

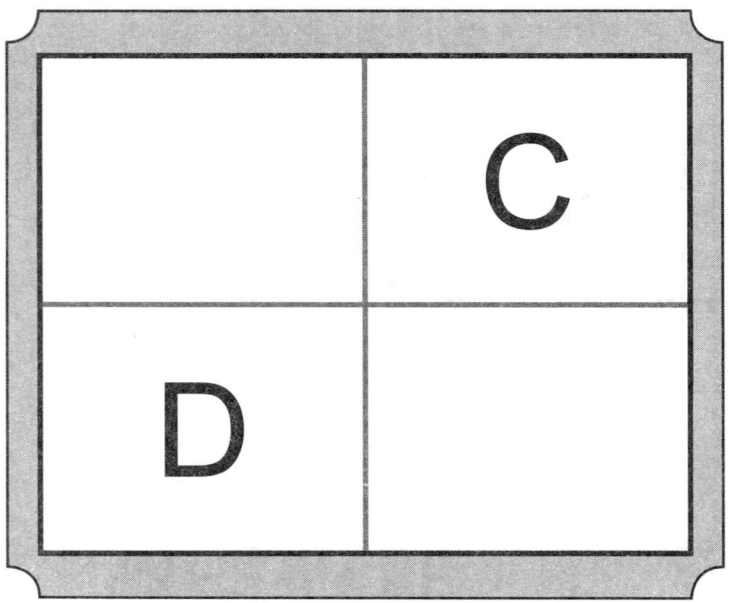

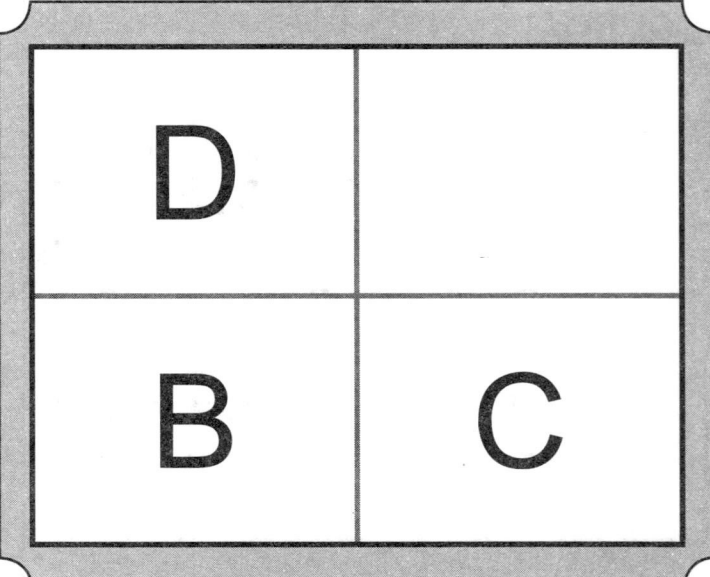

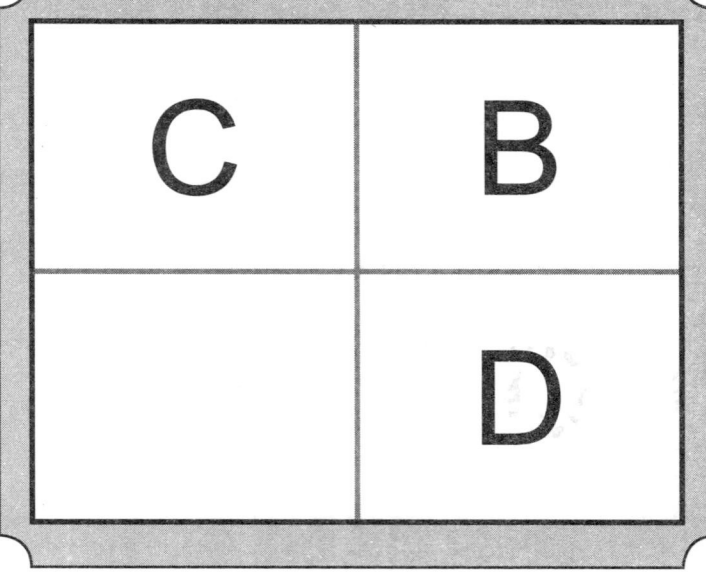

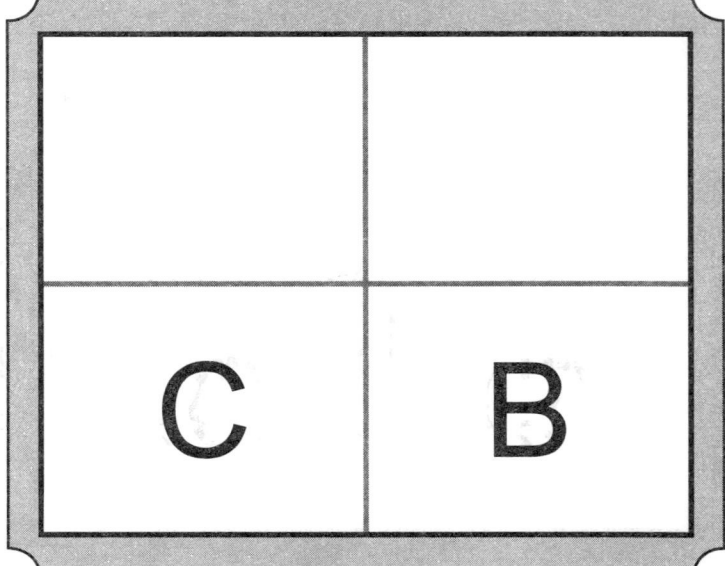

40 More Than One

Identify the picture in first column and then write their plurals in the second. One has been done for you. Take help from the Help Box.

Help Box

Snail Butterfly Bird Crab

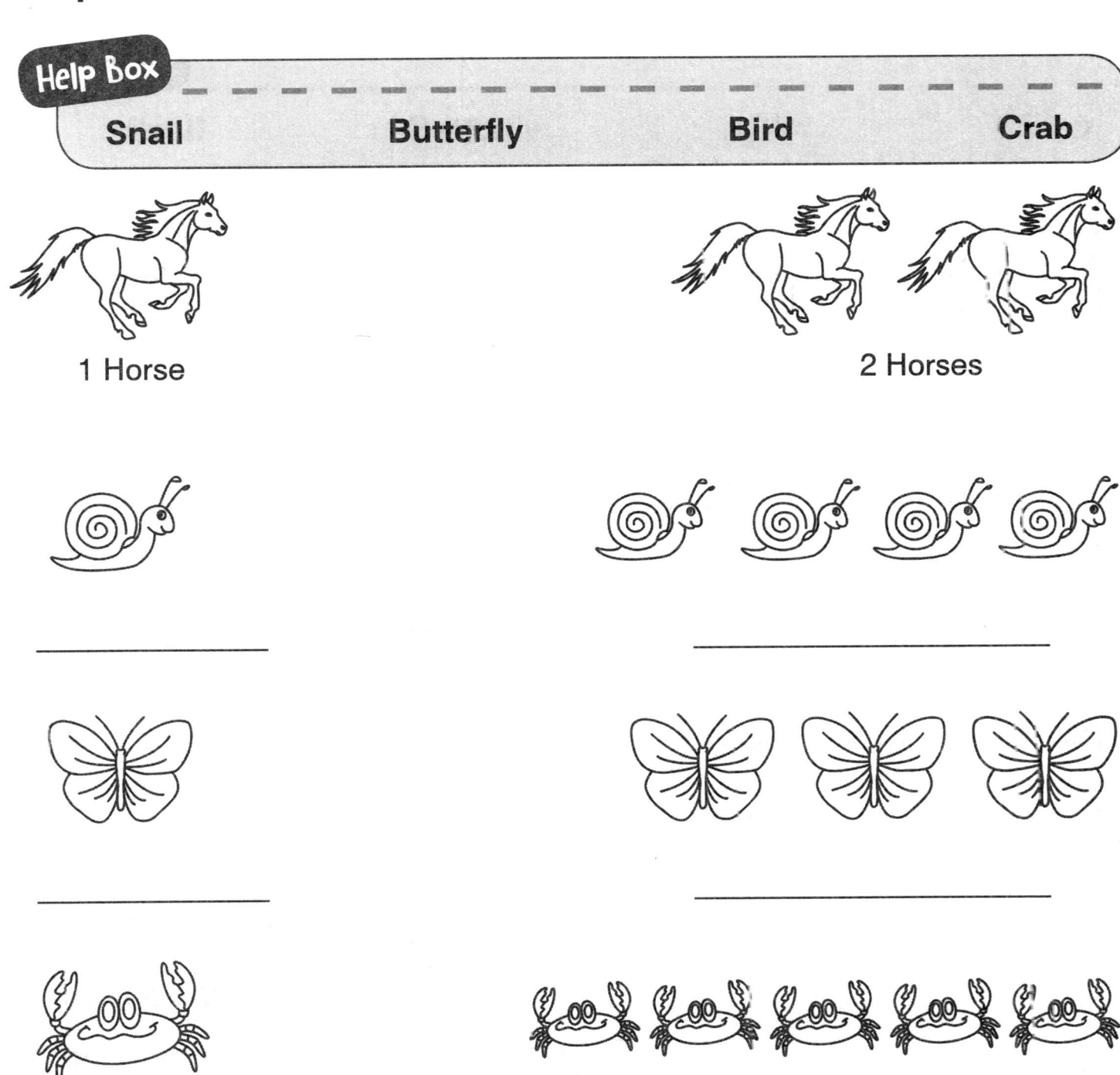

1 Horse   2 Horses

_____   _____

_____   _____

_____   _____

Date: _____   Teacher's Signature: _____

Search the Words

Read the poem and circle the words that end with 'ow' and 'eep'.

Little Boy Blue come blow

Your horn, the sheep's

In the meadow the

Cow's in the corn

But where is the boy who

Looks after the sheep?

He's under the haystack

fast asleep.

Will you wake him?

No, not I – for if I do,

He'll surely cry.

How many words end with 'ow'?

How many words end with 'eep'?

42   We Are the 'S' family

Circle the objects that begin with the letter 'S'.

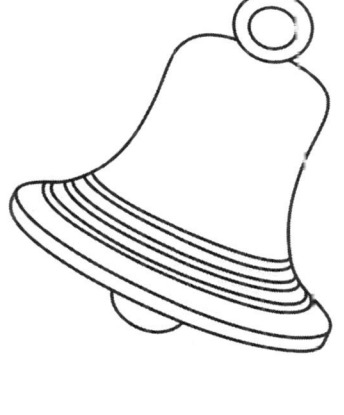

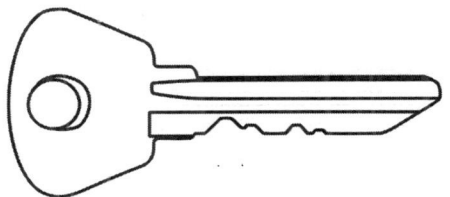

Date: _____   Teacher's Signature: _____

A of 'M'

Circle the objects that do not begin with the letter 'M'.

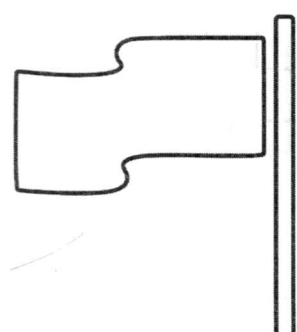

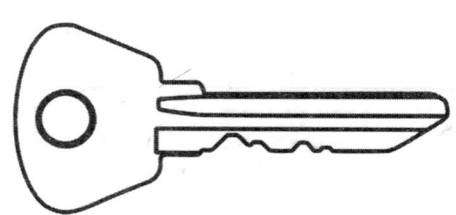

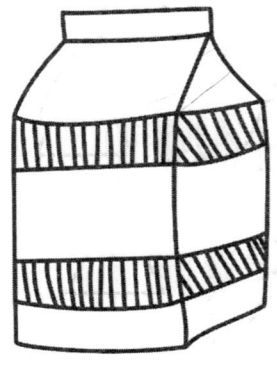

Stranger in the Row

Identify and write the name of the pictures. Circle the word in each group that doesn't start with the same sound as the letter at the end of each row. One has been done for you.

45 Playful Dog

Look at the picture given below. Colour it and use the words given in the Word Bank to create a sentence that describes the picture.

Word Bank

dog   the   holding   is   mouth   The   slipper   in   his

She Is My Sister

Look at the picture given below. Complete the sentence using one of the words from the Help Box.

Help Box

No   Not   Do   Don't

_____ tease your sister.

Date: _____   Teacher's Signature: _____

47 I Live in a Jungle

Look at the picture given below. Choose a correct word from the Help Box to complete the sentence.

Help Box

biggest   bigger   big   small

The rhino is _____ than the mice.

Date: _____   Teacher's Signature: _____

My Name is Lily

Lily wants to say something. Select a suitable word from the Help Box and help Lily complete the sentence.

I am Lily. My eyes are black. I have _____ hair.

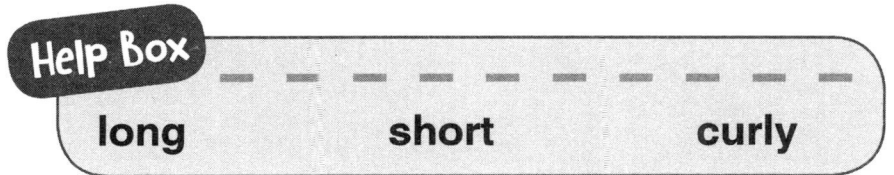

Help Box: long   short   curly

49 Ants in a Row

Ants are hard working insects. They always walk in rows. Count the ants in the rows and complete the sentence.

We are _____ ants walking in rows.

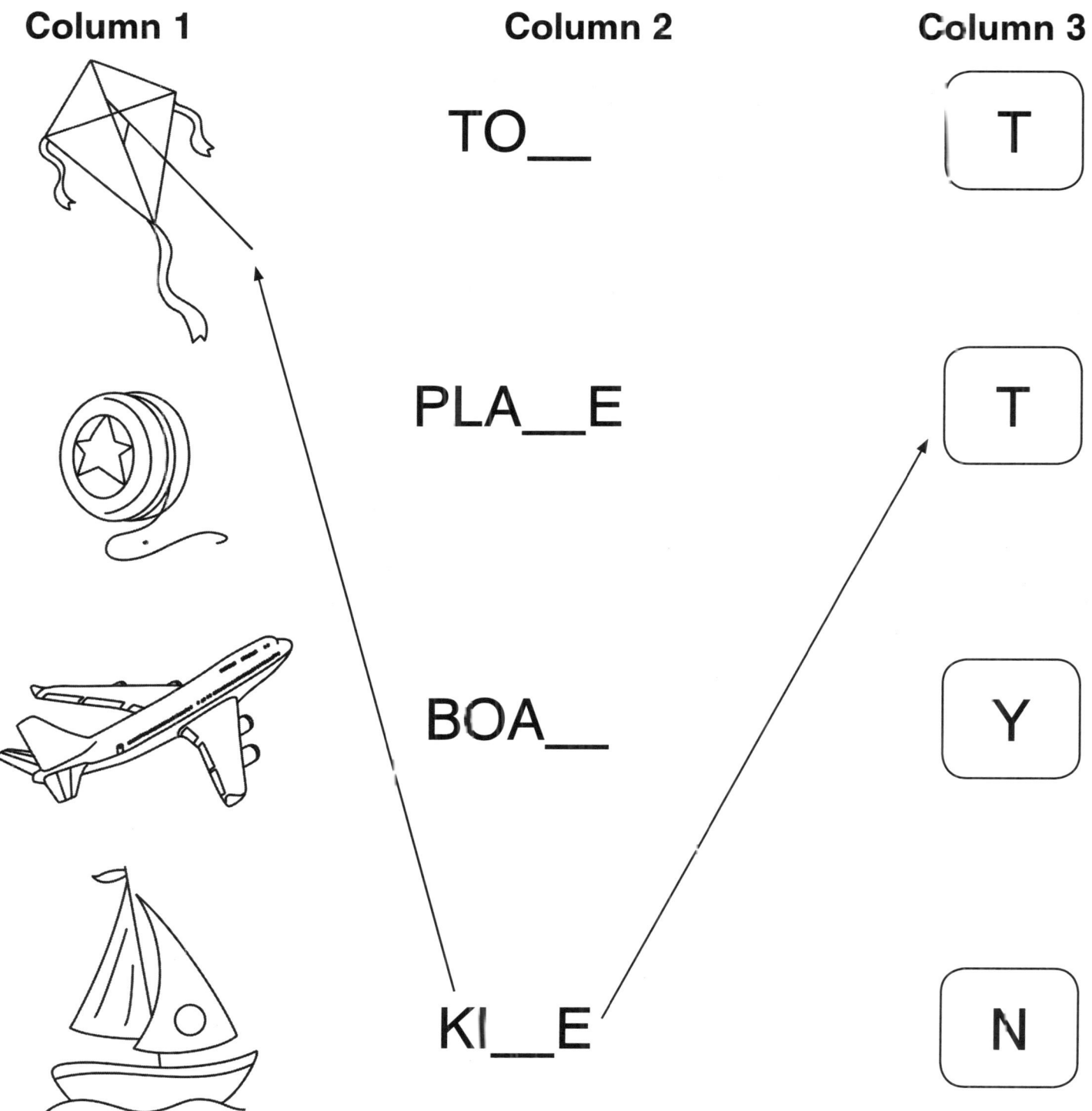

51 Use Only A, B, and C

Use only three capital letters, A, B and C to complete the following words. One has been done for you, trace the letter.

Bike

ee

ake

pple

at

nt

Date: _____ Teacher's Signature: _____

Beginning Letter

Match the pictures with the beginning letter of their names.

F

G

U

I

B

53 Tracing 'Have'

Trace each letter of the word 'have' in each line. Complete the sentence by filling the word 'have'.

have

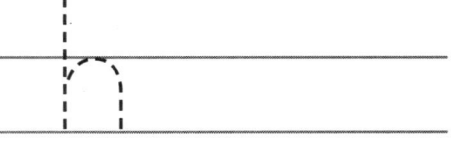
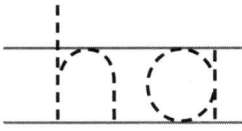

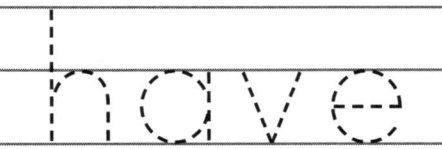

_____

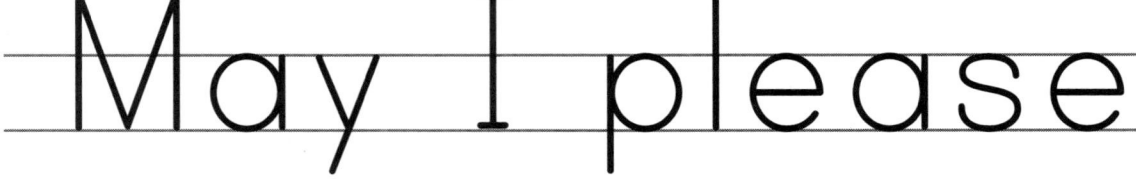

May I please

_____ some cake?

We Live in Water

Look at the pictures of water animals here. Colour them using different colours.

Identify any one water animal and write its name._____

Date: _____   Teacher's Signature: _____

55 How Many Times?

Read the poem and then fill in the blanks.

The ants go marching one by one.

Hoorah! Hoorah!

The ants go marching one by one.

Hoorah! Hoorah!

The ants go marching one by one;

The little one stops to suck his thumb,

And they all go marching down into the ground

To get out of the rain.

Boom, boom, boom, boom!

Ants march _____ times.

The little ant stops _____ time.

Date: _____   Teacher's Signature: _____

56   'F' for Fox

Look at the picture and read the words given below. Identify the two letters that are common between the two words.

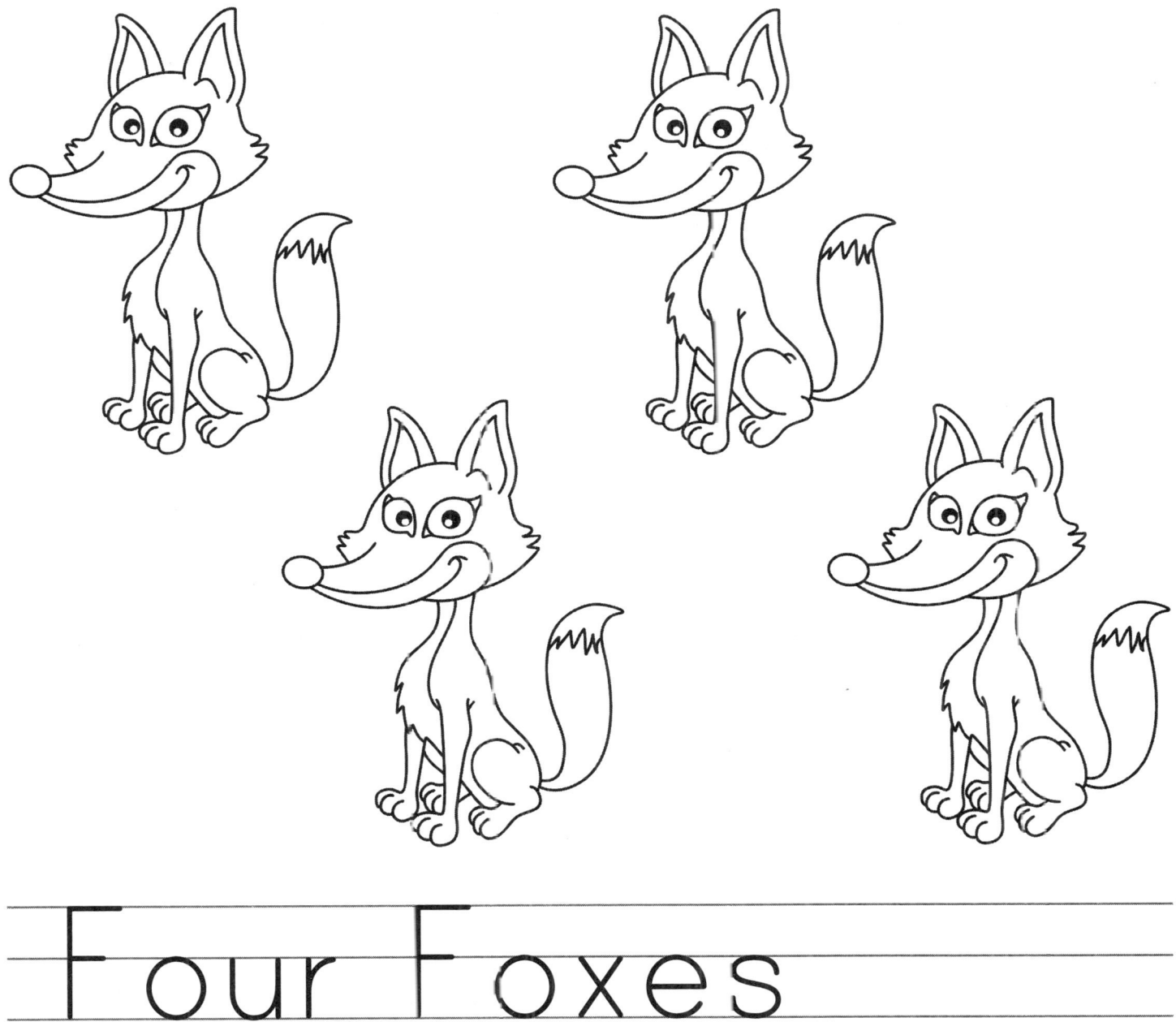

Four Foxes

The two common letters are _____ and _____.

Date: _____

57   I Am Falling Down

Read the following rhyme carefully. In the rhyme, there is something that is falling down. What is that?

    London Bridge is falling down,

    Falling down, falling down,

    London Bridge is falling down,

    My Fair Lady.

The object that is falling down is the _____.

Date: _____   Teacher's Signature: _____

58 We Are Two

Name the animals in the rhyme.

Pussy cat, pussy cat,

Where have you been?

"I've been to London to

Look at the Queen."

Pussy cat, pussy cat,

What did you there?

"I frightened a little mouse

Under the chair."

1. _____
2. _____

Date: _____

Teacher's Signature: _____

59 It's Christmas Time!

It's Christmas! Decorate the picture according to your imagination. Use different colours and add other decorative material to make it more beautiful.

Date: _____

Teacher's Signature: _____

Who Am I?

60

I am a reptile. I crawl on walls. Choose the correct letter from the words given below and fill the missing letter in the spelling of my name.

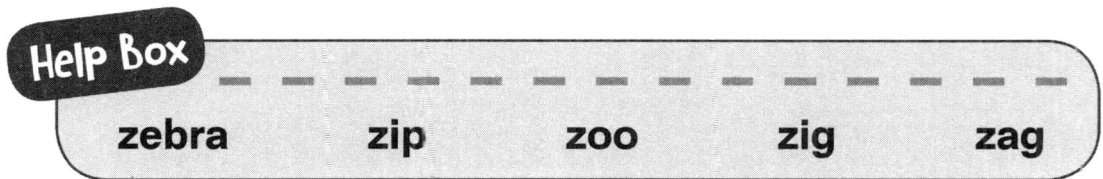

Help Box

zebra   zip   zoo   zig   zag

_l_ _i_ _____ _a_ _r_ _d_

Date: _____   Teacher's Signature: _____

67 The Insect Puzzle

Look at the pictures and complete the crossword.

Across

1. Snail

3. Ant

5. Butterfly

7. Bee

Down

2. Ladybird

6. Beetle

Connect the Dots

Connect the dots to complete the picture. Identify the object in the picture.

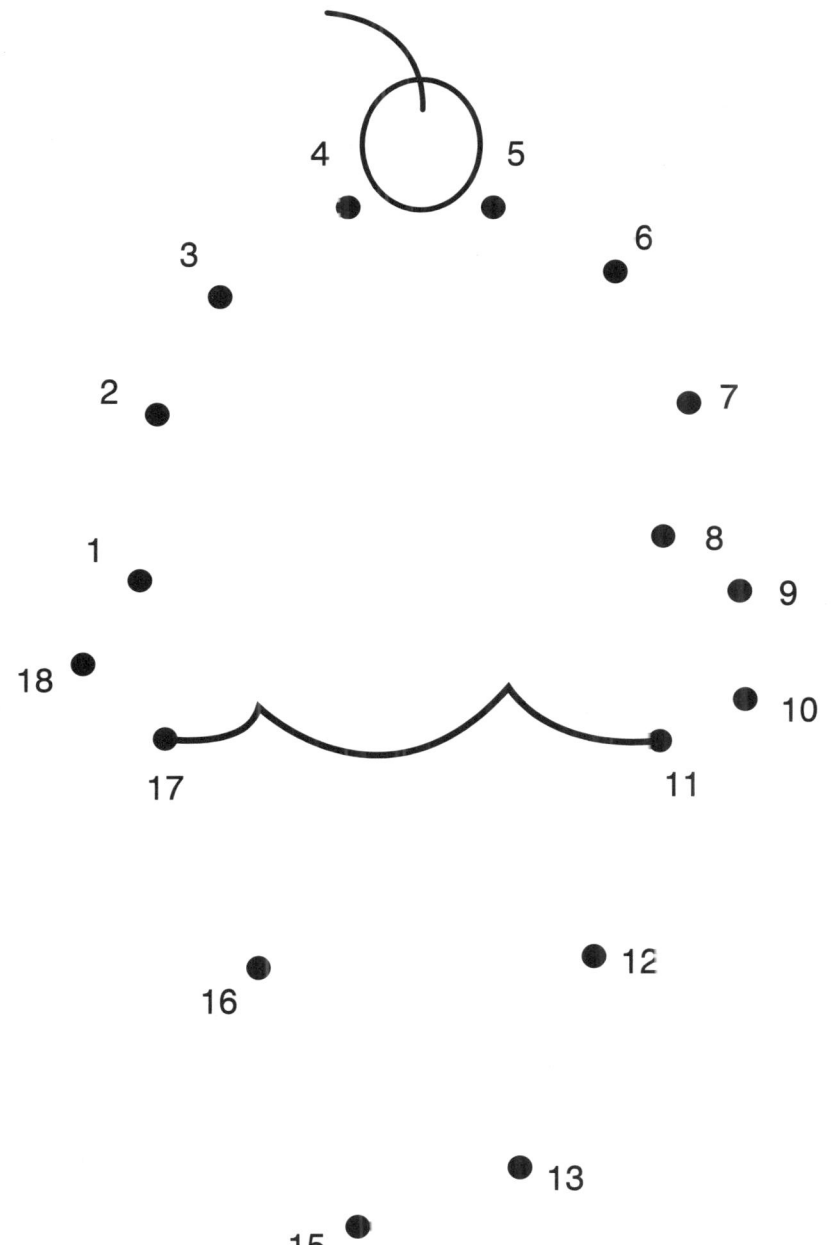

This is an _____.

Date: _____ Teacher's Signature: _____

63 I Make You Strong

Connect the dots from 1 to 10 to reveal the picture. Identify the object in the picture.

Hint: Its name starts with the letter 'E'.

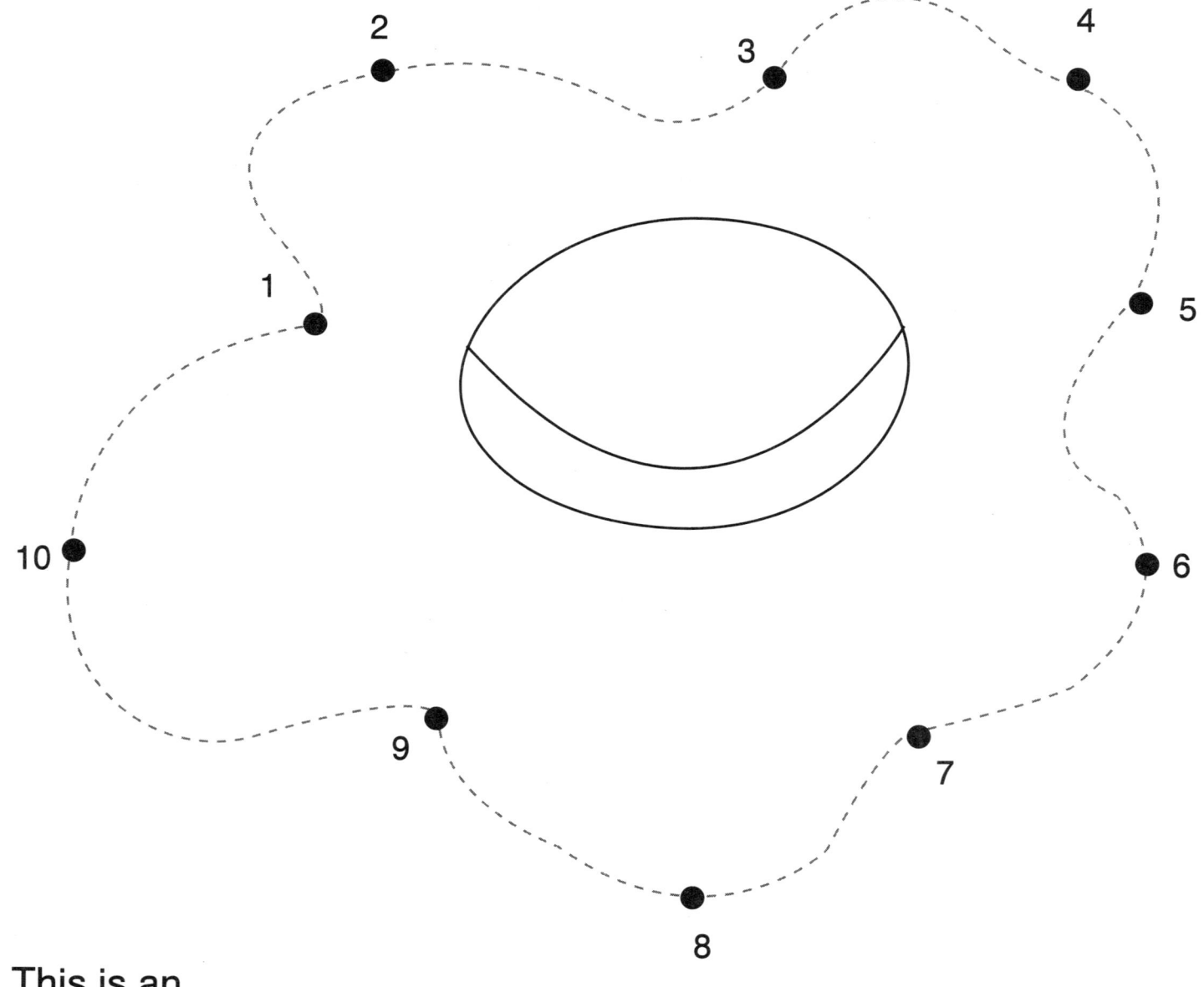

This is an _____.

Date: _____

Teacher's Signature: _____

I Love My Grandparents

Look at the picture given below. Colour the picture and write the name of your grandparents.

65   I Love This Taste

Different foods have different tastes. Look at some of the food pictures in the box and make a smiley in front of those you like to eat.

A. Strawberry

B. Lemon

C. Bitter Gourd

D. Potato Chips

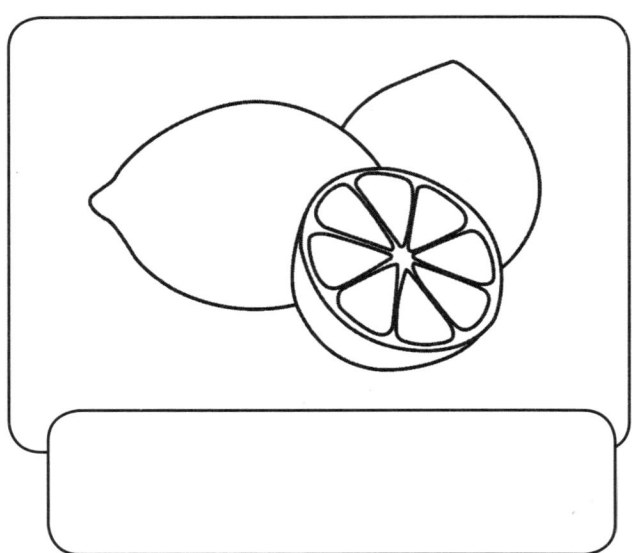

Date: _____

Teacher's Signature: _____

I Can Hear This

See the pictures given below. Colour the pictures of the objects that produce sound.

Colourful World

67

Colour the pictures and write the first letter of the names of these pictures.

Mirror, Mirror

Look at the mirror and draw the picture that you see in the mirror.

Date: _____ Teacher's Signature: _____

Eyes and Tongue

Eyes help us see and tongue helps us taste. Both the pictures here show the use of these two senses. Choose the correct answer from the Help Box and write in the space under each picture.

Help Box

I use my eyes.   I use my tongue.

70 Complete Me

Complete the pictures in the second column by drawing the missing parts of the pictures.

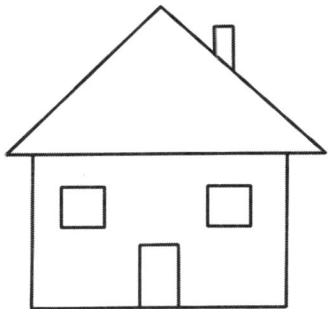
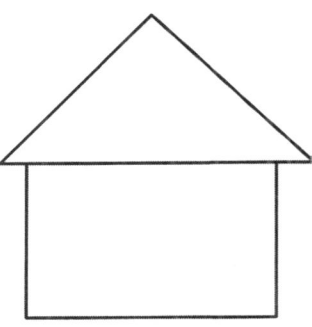

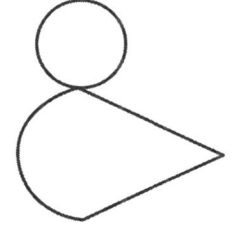

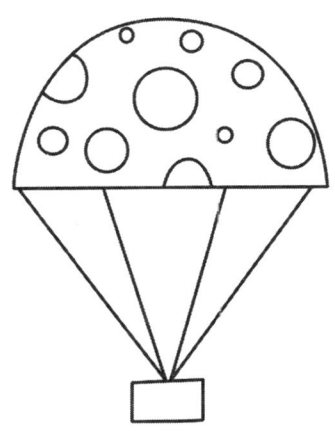

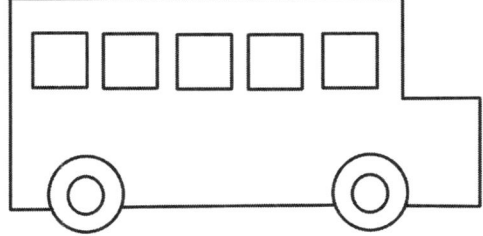

Date: _____   Teacher's Signature: _____

71 Incomplete Names

Read aloud the name of every picture. Fill the missing letter in the blank spaces with the help of the letters given in the boxes.

CA __   T

DO __   S

MOU __ E   N

A __ T   G

Date: _____   Teacher's Signature: _____

| 12 | **My Nickname** |

Identify the animal and give it a nickname. You can also colour the picture.

I am a _____.

My nickname is _____.

Date: _____ Teacher's Signature: _____

73 We Sound the Same

Match the rhyming words.

chain

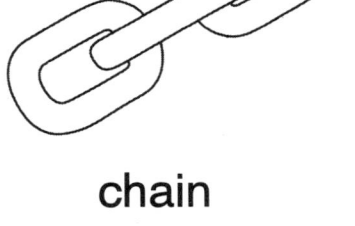
shoe

float

jug

flew

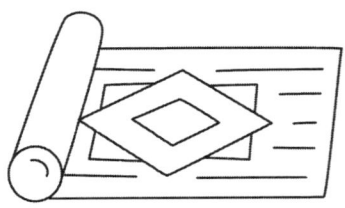
rug

boat

rain

74 I Love to Eat Leaves

Look at the picture given below. Use the words in the Help Box and complete the following sentences.

Help Box

| animal | neck | giraffe | jungle |

a. I am an _____.

b. I live in the _____.

c. I am called a _____.

d. I have a long _____.

75 Link the Pictures

Match the pictures with the correct sentences.

People wear so many layers of clothes in winters.

It is very hot in summer

We see colourful flowers in spring.

We see people with umbrellas in rainy season.

I Am a Healthy Food

Colour the pictures and answer the questions.

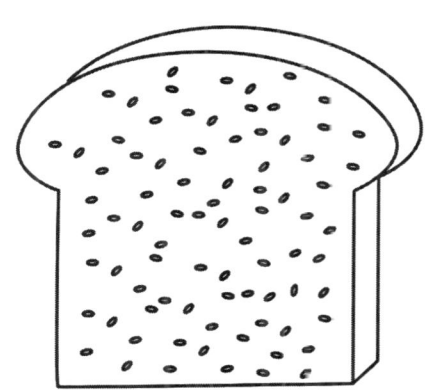

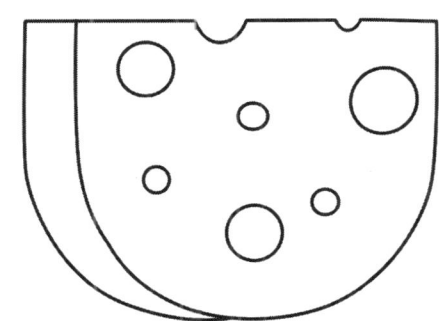

Are all these food items healthy? Choose.

a.   Yes   b. No

Which one of these is your favourite food?_____

Which one of these is your least favourite food? _____

Date: _____

77 We Live in Same Pond

Colour the picture. Complete the sentence with the help of the Help Box.

Help Box: water   air   land

Fishes swim in _____.

Date: _____   Teacher's Signature: _____

78 Fruits or Vegetables?

Identify the fruits and vegetables in the given picture. Write 'F' around the fruits and 'V' around the vegetables.

_____

_____

_____

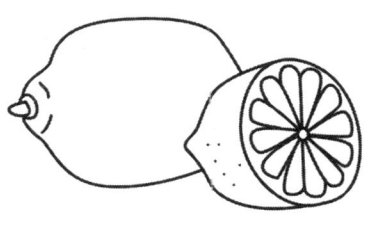
_____

_____

_____

_____

_____

_____

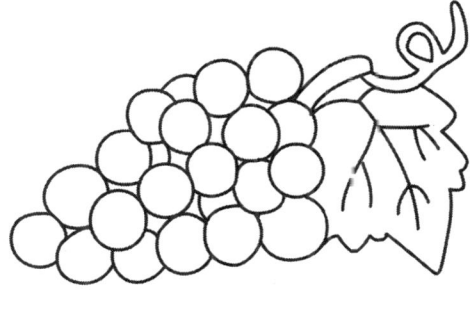
_____

Date: _____ Teacher's Signature: _____

79 Chug, Chug on the Track

Complete the drawing by connecting the dotted lines and colour it. What is this?

I am a _____.

80 My Dream Playground

Choose your favourite playground equipment from the pictures and draw your dream playground.

Date: _____ Teacher's Signature: _____

Primary Colours

These are the three primary colours. Read their names and colour the crayon sticks.

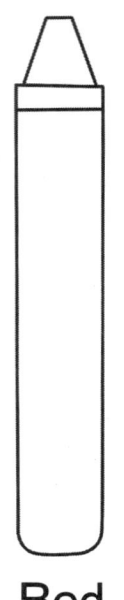 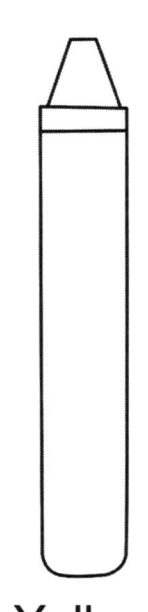 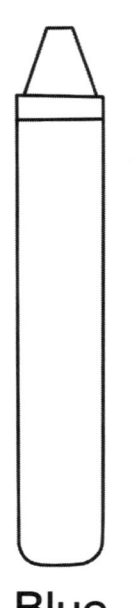

Red Yellow Blue

Now colour the following objects with the three primary colours.

Date: _____ Teacher's Signature: _____

82 Smell and Tell

Nose helps us smell things. Look at the pictures in the box and connect them with the type of smell they have.

Note: Get help from a parent or an elder if required.

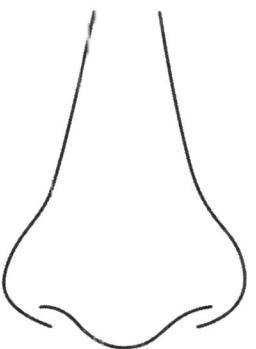

Stinky	
Sweet	
Floral	
Spicy	

83 It's Me!

Stick a picture of yourself when you were a baby. Can you recognise yourself? Fill in your information below.

When I was 6 month old, I looked like this: 06

My birthday is on: _____

I started eating when I was (ask you mamma about it):

_____

Date: _____   Teacher's Signature: _____

My Lovely House

Take help from your elders and the Help Box to complete the story titled 'My Lovely House'.

Help Box

very big,   small,   yellow and white,   green,   two,   my school

My house is _____.

My front door is _____.

The colour of the walls are _____ _____.

My backyard is _____.

There are _____ rooms in my house.

My house is near _____.

85 Count in the Rhyme

Read the poem and count how many times do the words head, shoulders, knees and toes appear in it.

Head and shoulders knees and toes

Knees and toes

Head and shoulders knees and toes

Knees and toes

And eyes and ears

And mouth and nose

Head and shoulders knees and toes

Knees and toes

Head: _____

Shoulders: _____

Knees: _____

Toes: _____

Date: _____   Teacher's Signature: _____

Not in the Ocean

Cross (x) the pictures of animals that are not part of the ocean.

87 I Am a Fireman

Match A and B to complete the rhyme.

A

1. Fireman saves lives every

2. Hear sirens? They are on the

3. Safety first is what they

4. So learn your fire safety rules

B

a. today

b. say

c. day

d. way

Space Scientist

Which statement is true about the corresponding image? Mark (✓) for true ones and (x) for false ones.

There is only one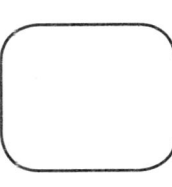

There is only one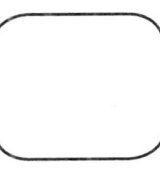

There is only one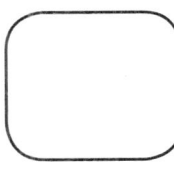

There is only one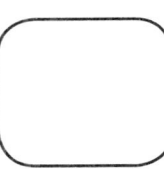

Date: _____   Teacher's Signature: _____

Find Us in the Kitchen

Unscramble the words in the first column and match with the pictures of the kitchen utensils.

ifkne ☐

onosp ☐

wolb ☐

nap ☐

rofk ☐

Date: _____ Teacher's Signature: _____

90 In Order

Complete the following sequences by filling missing letters.

LM__ XY__

JK__ UV__

__BC __OP

__RS __EF

Date: ________ Teacher's Signature: ________

In the Nature

Match the following pictures with the correct sentence.

   The flowers bloom.

   The moon shines.

   The sun is bright.

   A dog eats.

   A cat sleeps.

   The leaf falls.

Toy Store

Look at the pictures and then answer the questions.

How many toys do not have wheels? _____

How many toys have wheels? _____

How many are toy animals? _____

How many are musical toys? _____

Date: _____   Teacher's Signature: _____

Shoe Store

Look at the pictures and then answer the questions.

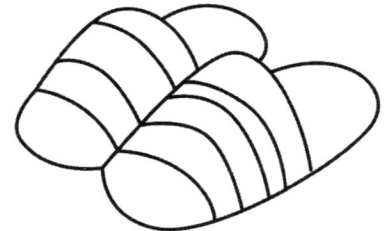

Number of bathroom slippers   _____

Number of boots   _____

Number of footwears that are not boots   _____

Number of sport shoes   _____

Ronny the Kitten

I am Ronny, a little kitten. Observe my expression and answer the questions with Yes or No.

Am I angry?   _____

Am I afraid?   _____

Am I happy?   _____

Am I crying?   _____

Am I sad?   _____

Date: _____   Teacher's Signature: _____

95 We Are All Living Things

Look at the picture given below. They all are living things. What do they all need? Choose correct options from the Help Box and write in each box.

Help Box

Fruits   Buns   Clothes   Air   Soup   Water   Milk   Sunlight

Quack! Quack! Quack!

Read the rhyme and fill in the blank space.

5 is for five ducks

Five little ducks went swimming one day,

Over the hill and far away.

Mother duck said, "Quack! Quack! Quack!"

But only four little ducks came back.

Four little ducks went swimming one day,

Over the hill and far away.

Mother duck said, "Quack! Quack! Quack!"

But only three little ducks came back.

Three little ducks went swimming one day,

Over the hill and far away.

The Mother duck says 'Quack! Quack! Quack!' _____ times.

Date: _____   Teacher's Signature: _____

97 We Go to School

Arrange A, B, C and D in the correct order to complete the picture. You can arrange it by drawing line to the correct part in the main picture.

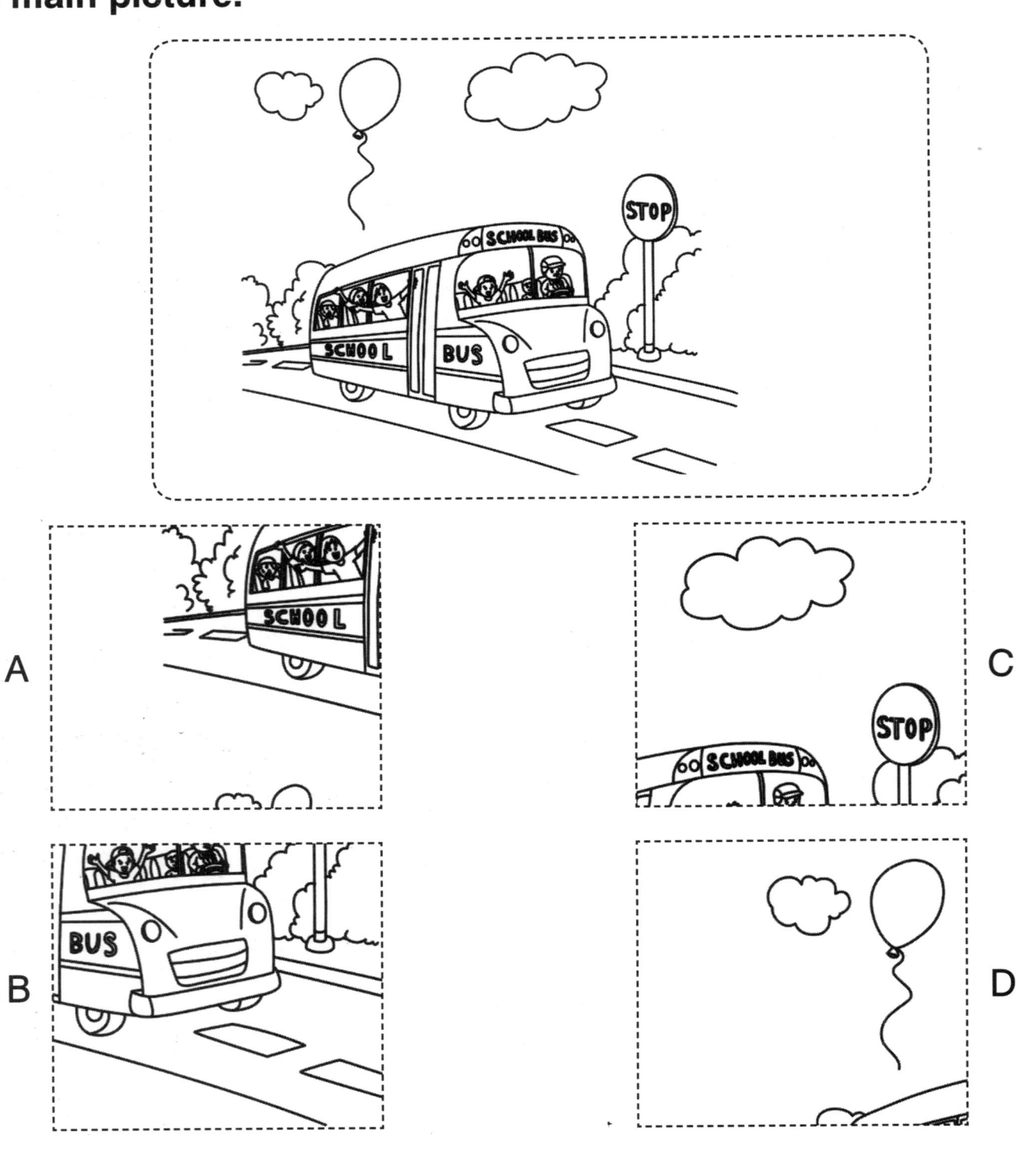

98 Boy in the Garden

Look at the picture and complete the sentence using the correct words from the Help Box.

Help Box

He	**She**	**His**	**Her**

__________ is a boy.

Date: ____________ Teacher's Signature: ____________

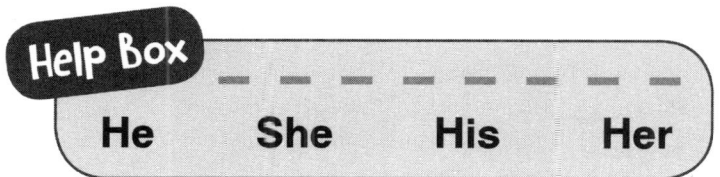

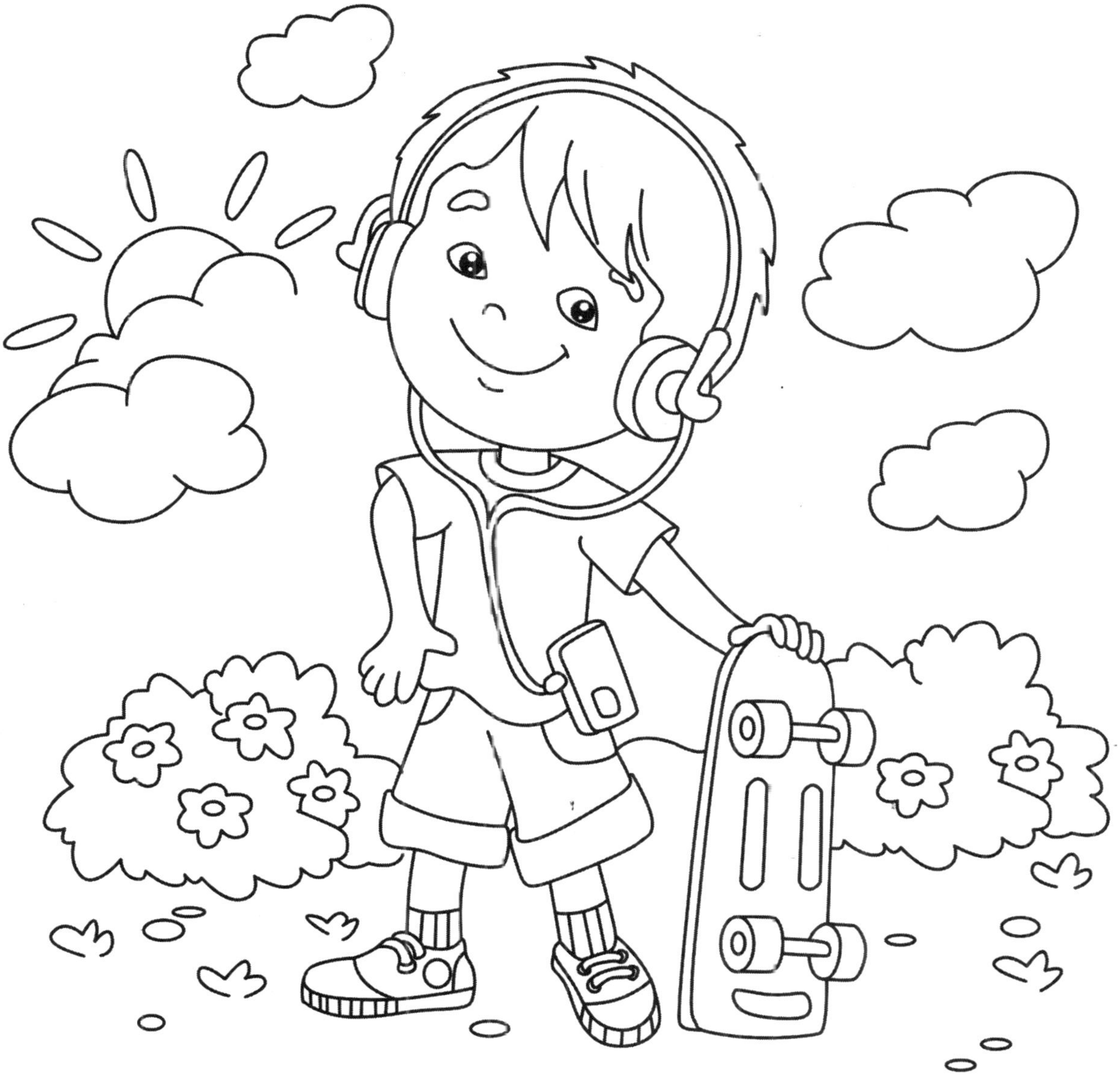

I Am Smiling

99

Identify the animal in the picture and write what it is doing.

I am a _____.

I am _____.

Date: _____

Teacher's Signature: _____

Make a Word

Write down two simple words with each alphabet.

W

I

N

T

E

R

Date: _____   Teacher's Signature: _____

101 School Kit

Which is the one thing given here that is useful but can be dangerous, if used carelessly?

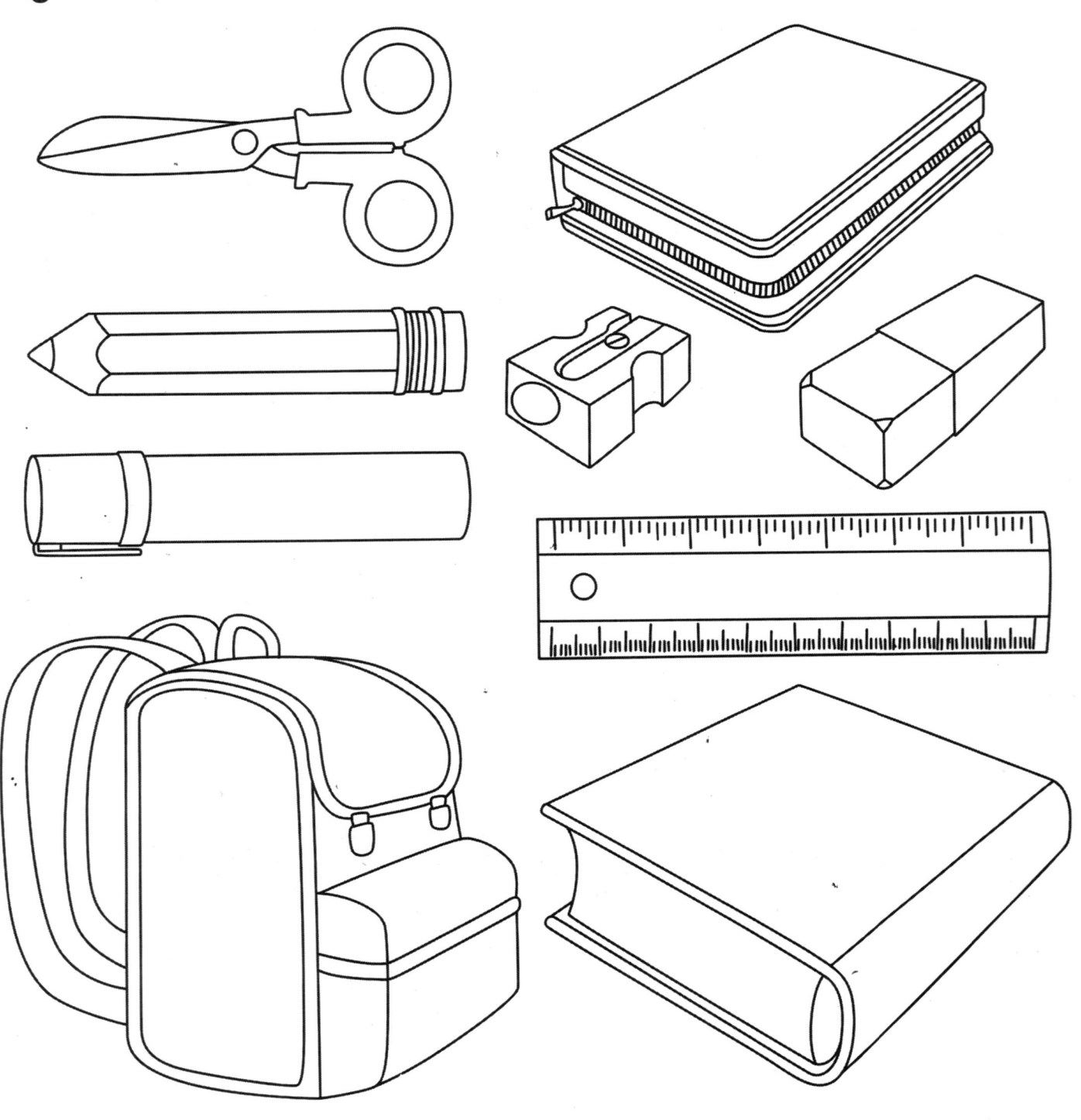

Write the name of the object. _____

Date: _____   Teacher's Signature: _____

102 Predict the Weather

Choose the correct option from the box to complete these weather-related words.

   ___ain    i

   ___ce   r

   ___un   c

   ___loud   s

Hungry Baby Bear

Mamma bear wants to feed the baby bear. Help Mamma bear find her way to baby bear.

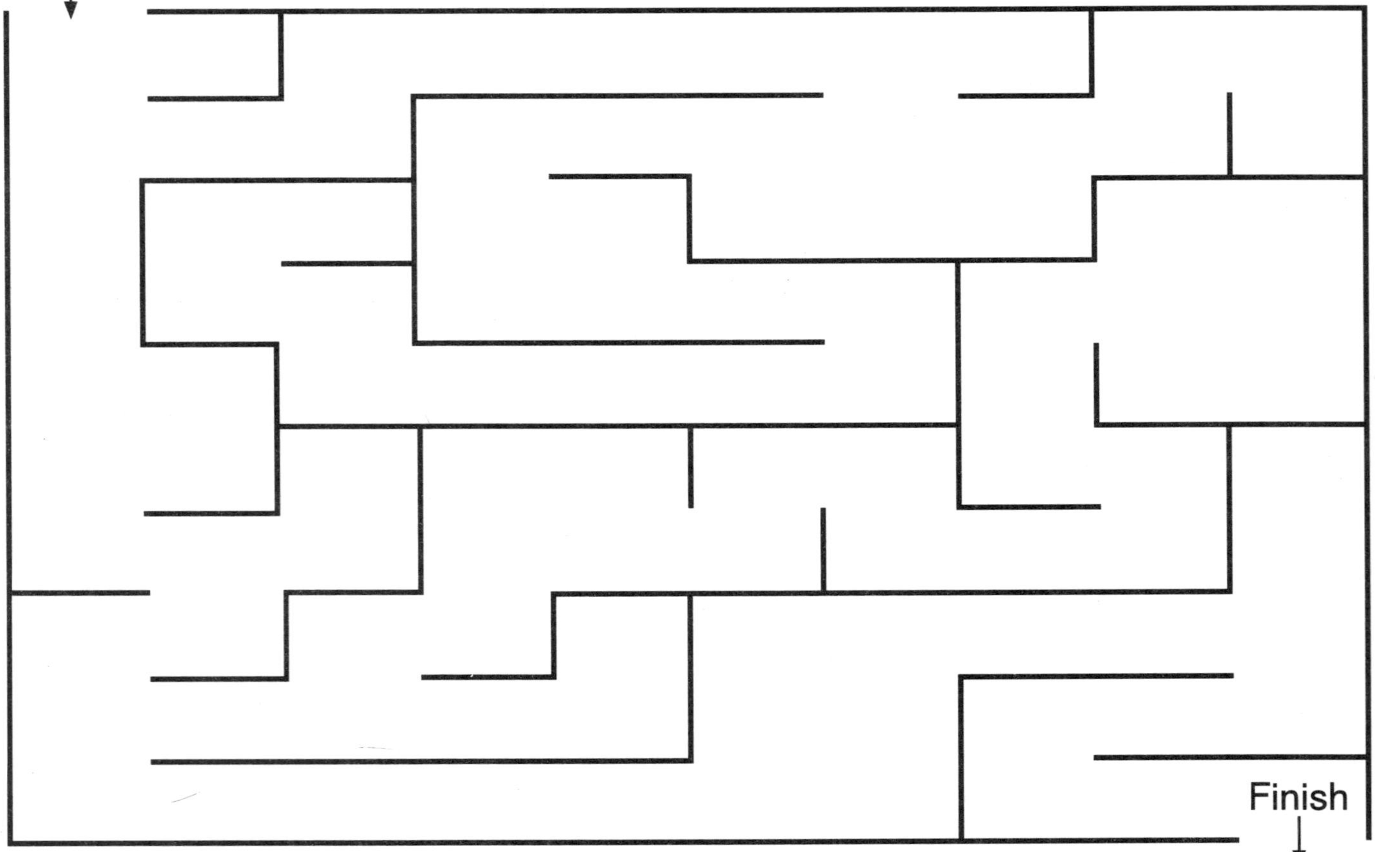

Start ↓

Finish ↓

Date: _____

Teacher's Signature: _____

104 Words with 'An'

Add 'an' after every given letter and make some meaningful words. One of them has been done for you. Add picture cutouts or draw the picture for some of the new words.

v	van
f	
m	
r	
c	

Date: _____   Teacher's Signature: _____

105 Picture Rhyming with Cat

Colour only those pictures that rhyme with the word 'cat'.

I Sound Different

Circle the picture whose name does not sound like the names of other pictures.

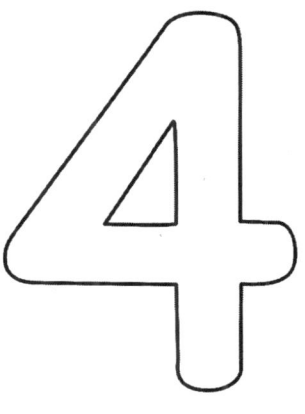
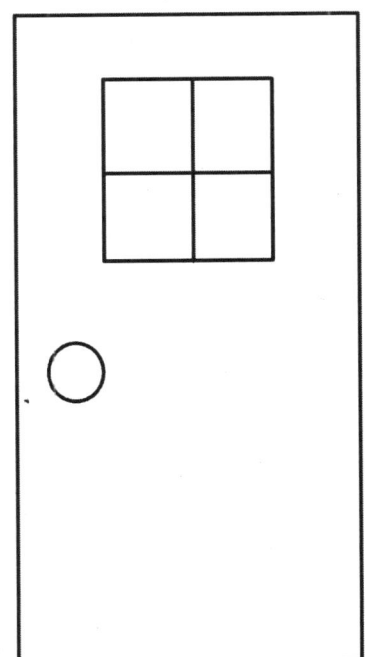
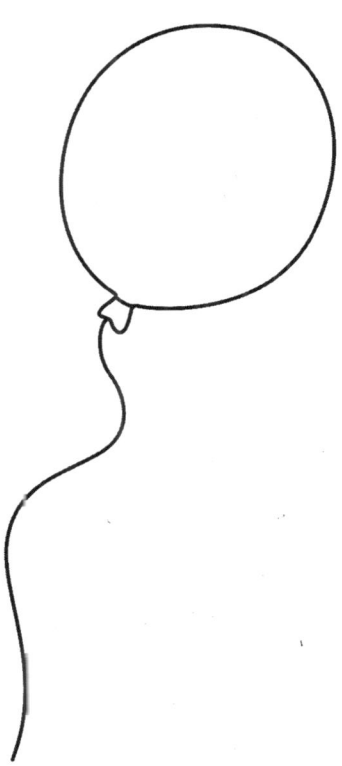

107 I Rhyme with Socks

Colour only those pictures that rhyme with the word 'socks'.

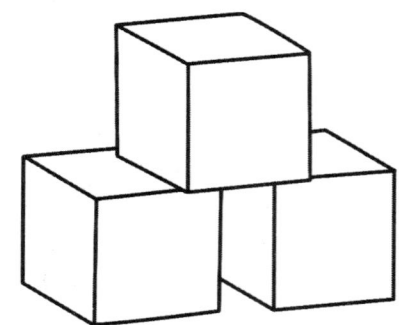

Three Small Letters

Use the three small letters 'a', 'e' and 'u' to complete these words.

b __ e

c __ n

s __ n

Complete the Words

Use the three small letters 'a', 'e' and 'o' to complete these words.

v _ n

h _ n

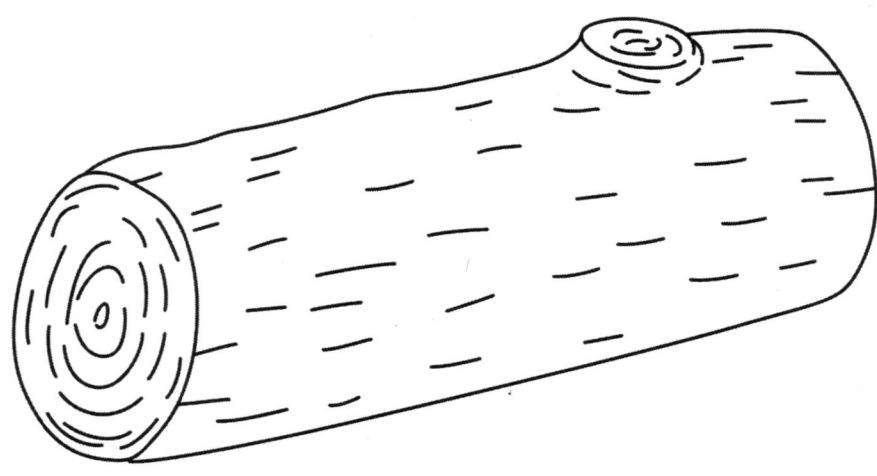

l _ g

School Sudoku

Solve the sudoku by filling the correct word in the blank squares. The words—pencil, car, scissors and bag—must appear only once in each row, column, and block.

	Pencil		Bag
Bag	Scissors	Pencil	Car
	Car		Scissors
Scissors	Bag	Car	Pencil

Date: _____ Teacher's Signature: _____

111 Parts of a Tree

Use the words given in the Help Box below to label the parts of a tree.

Help Box: Leaf   Branch   Fruit   Trunk   Root

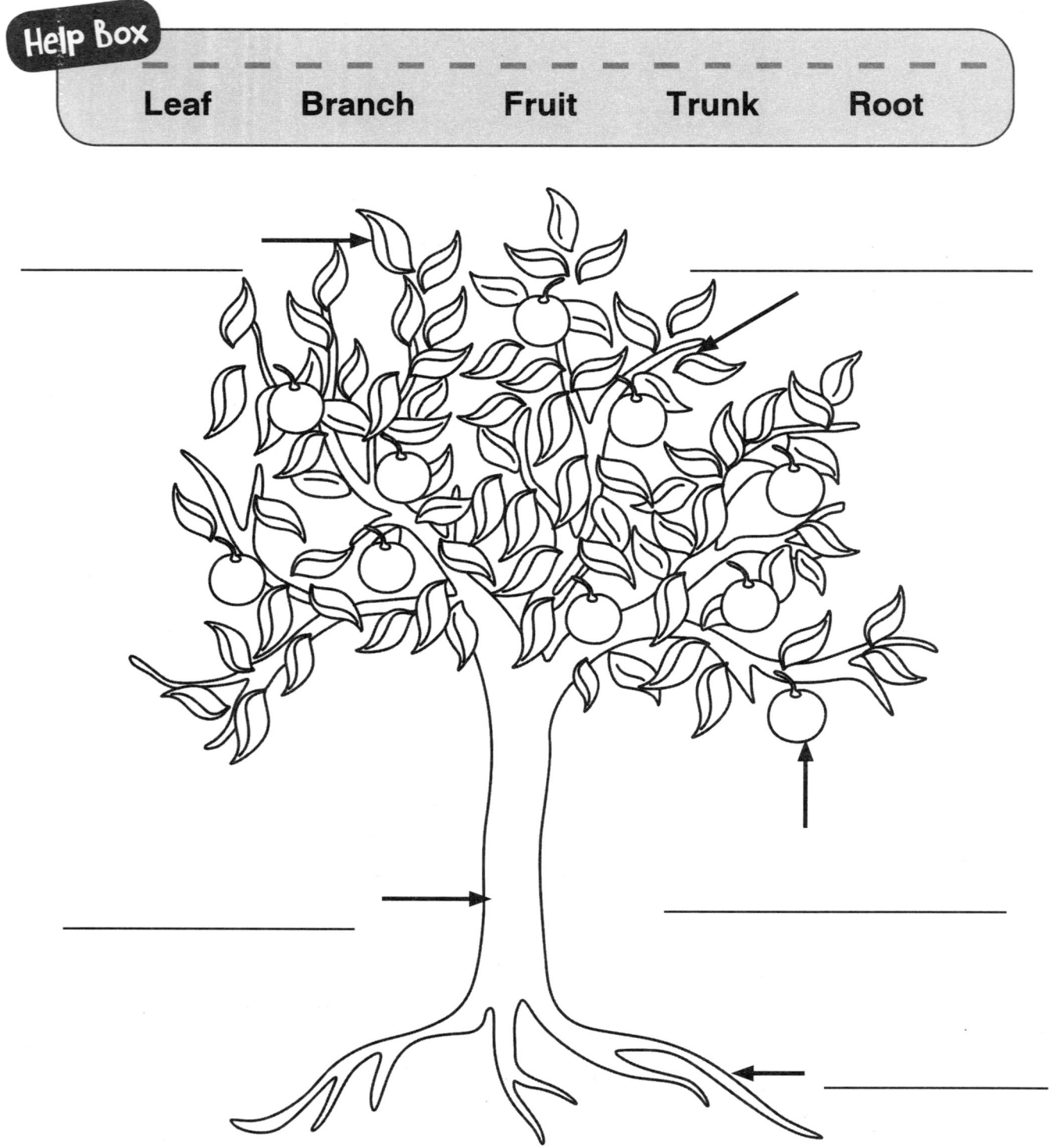

M, N and O

Use the letters 'M', 'N', and 'O' to complete the following words.

__ANGO

__WL

__EST

__STRICH

__AIL

113. We Are in the Sea

Colour the places where a number or a letter is written and see what is hidden behind. It is related to the sea.

Use same colour for one number/letter. For example: colour spaces marked '1' in blue.

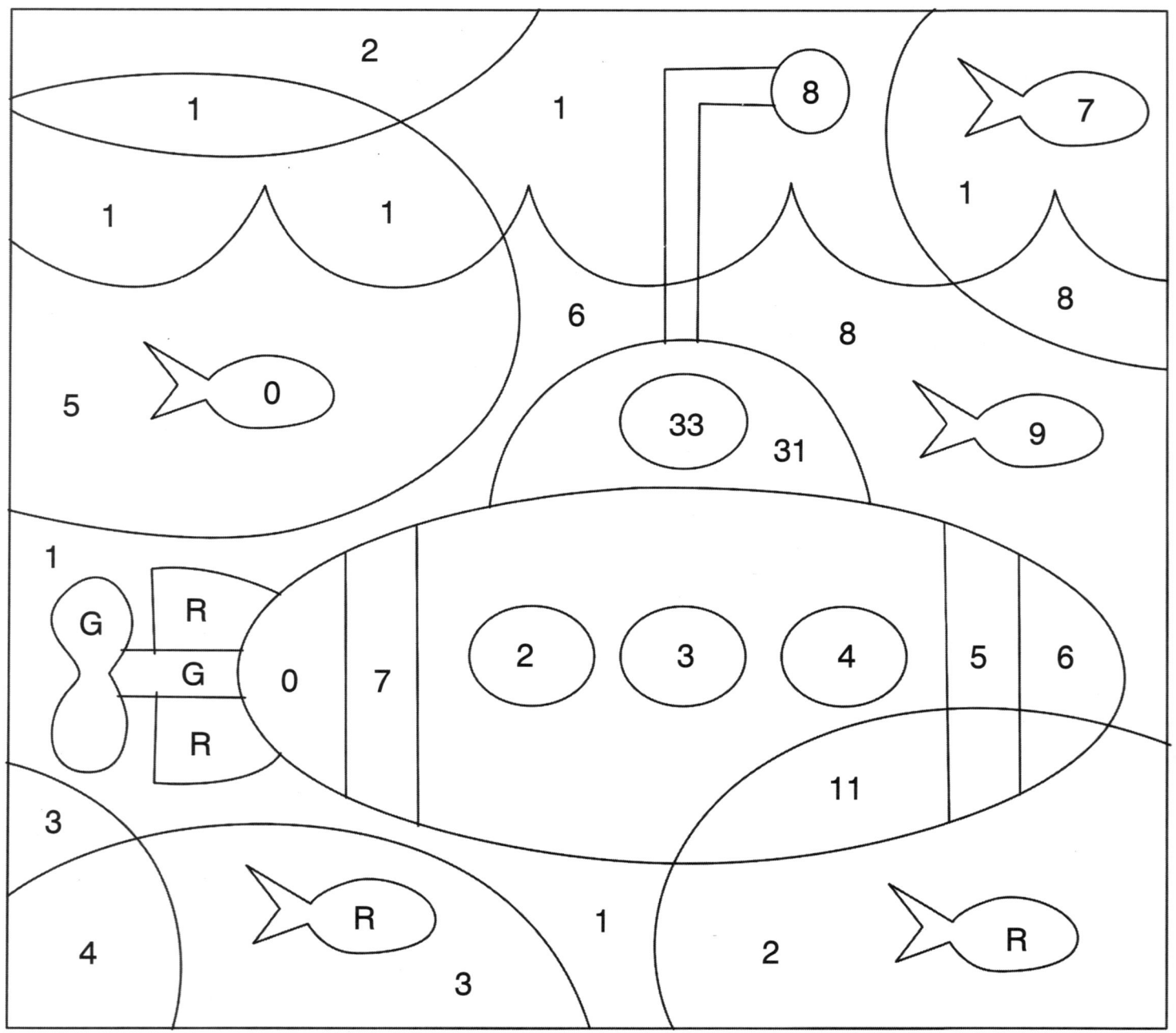

Starting with 'H'

114

Connect the dots with letter 'H'. Start from the star.

Hint: My name starts with H. People use me to spray water.

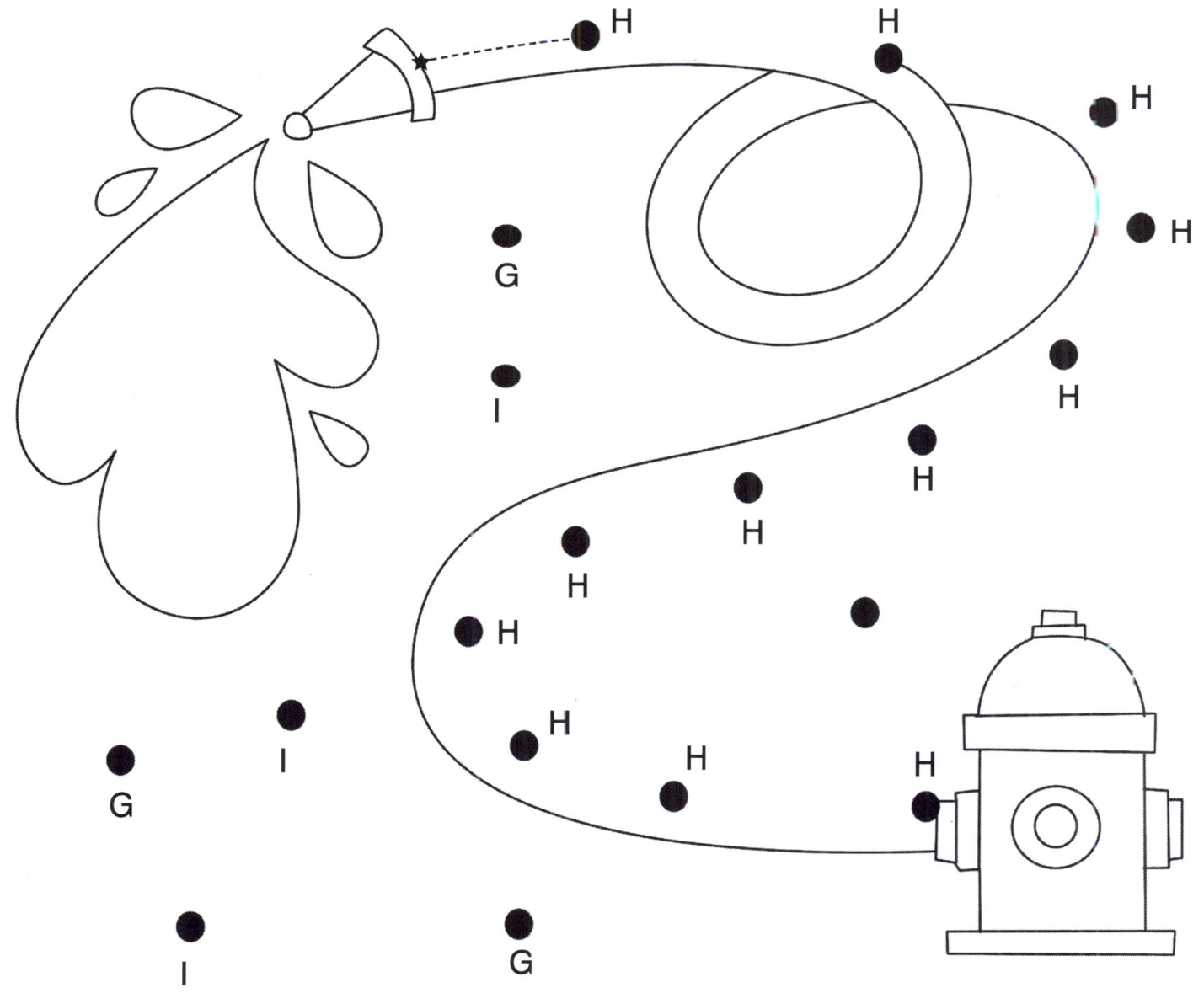

115 What Is It Doing?

Identify the animal, what is it doing and what is its mood like?

Position clues: running, sitting, standing

Mood clues: sad, happy, angry

I am a _____.

Mood: I am _____.

Position: I am _____.

Date: _____   Teacher's Signature: _____

I Am a Puzzle Master!

Complete the given puzzle with the help of the picture clues.

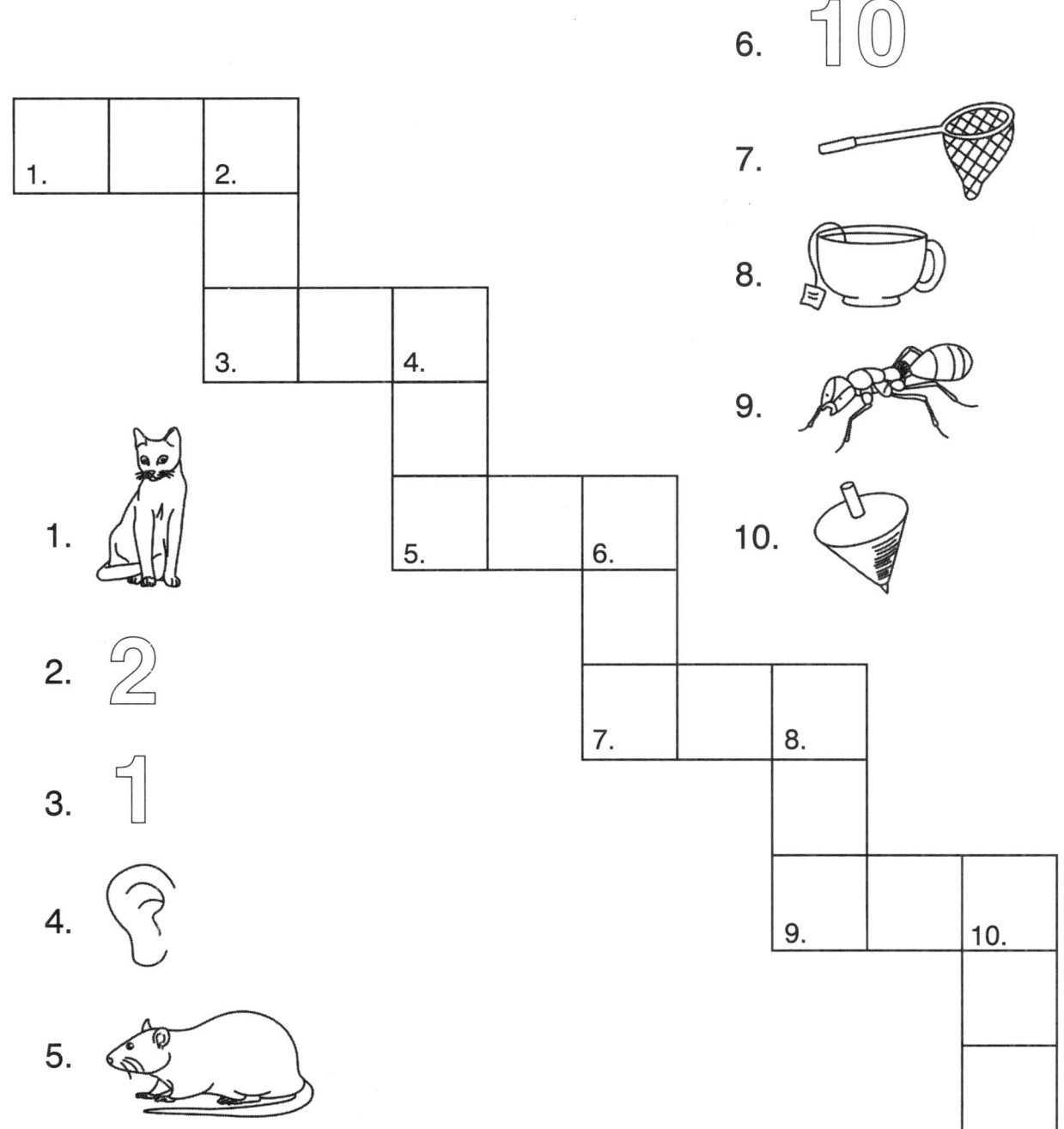

117 Writing Sight Word

Trace and complete the sight word.

p

play

play

I am learning to _____ football.

Complete Me

Fill the missing letters using words from the Help Box.

Help Box

spring   grass   egg   flower   basket

spr__ng

gr__ss

__gg

b__sk__t

fl__w__r

The missing letters are

☐ ☐ ☐ ☐

119 Colouring Small Letters

Colour the grids containing small letters.

A	b	N	M	d	h	F	D	h	w
q	G	t	y	u	K	a	C	n	U
A	D	f	g	H	q	G	g	y	z
b	N	m	Q	a	U	i	o	p	Y
S	f	g	t	R	E	W	v	B	n
A	h	j	g	g	A	R	E	w	Q
H	F	d	h	j	k	l	s	G	H
J	m	T	y	U	t	o	S	A	d
F	g	h	j	k	L	d	y	a	D
s	e	y	t	N	m	z	a	q	p

Word Count

Count the number of words in each sentence given below. Write the number in the blank spaces. One has been done for you.

1. The cat sleeps.   ___3___

2. My mom loves me.   _____

3. We like to listen to music.   _____

4. Can you help me with my homework?   _____

5. I saw a bear.   _____

6. Tom loves winter.   _____

7. What is your name?   _____

8. There are many stars in the sky.   _____

9. Rachel is very sick.   _____

10. The party was fun yesterday.   _____

Date: _____   Teacher's Signature: _____

121 Long and Short 'E' Sound

Letters have different sounds in different words. Identify the words with long and short 'E' sound. Circle the words that have long 'E' sound and strike out the words that have short 'E' sound.

1. her
2. egg
3. bee
4. read
5. feed
6. these
7. bread
8. see
9. head
10. flea
11. exit
12. chief
13. key
14. here
15. thief

Now and Then

Circle the things that are used in the present and cross those which were used in the past.

Become a Designer

Design and colour this soccer uniform.

124 Puzzle Your Brain

Search and circle all the words in the list below.

B	D	G	U	X	S	W	I	M	N
A	N	P	F	A	H	R	L	F	I
C	E	W	T	E	N	T	S	I	T
K	F	S	M	O	R	E	S	R	R
P	O	R	Y	I	N	G	Z	E	E
A	O	C	A	M	P	S	I	T	E
C	D	K	H	S	A	K	A	L	S
K	W	D	Z	Q	H	I	K	E	M

TENTS FOOD TREES

FIRE SWIM BACKPACK

Date: _____ Teacher's Signature: _____

125 Where Do I Move On?

Look at the pictures given below. These are things that help us move from one place to another.

Write:

'R' in front of the thing that moves on the road.

'W' for those that move on water

'A' for those that fly in air

___ ___

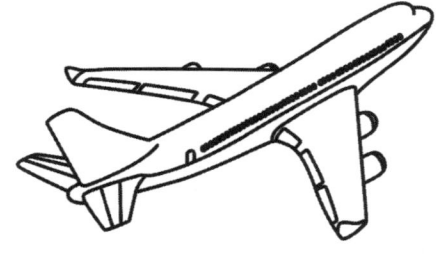 

___ ___

___ ___

Word Building Challenge

Look at the following pictures. Some of the letters are missing from their names. Complete the words using letters from the Help Box.

Help Box: A L F B G L O R A

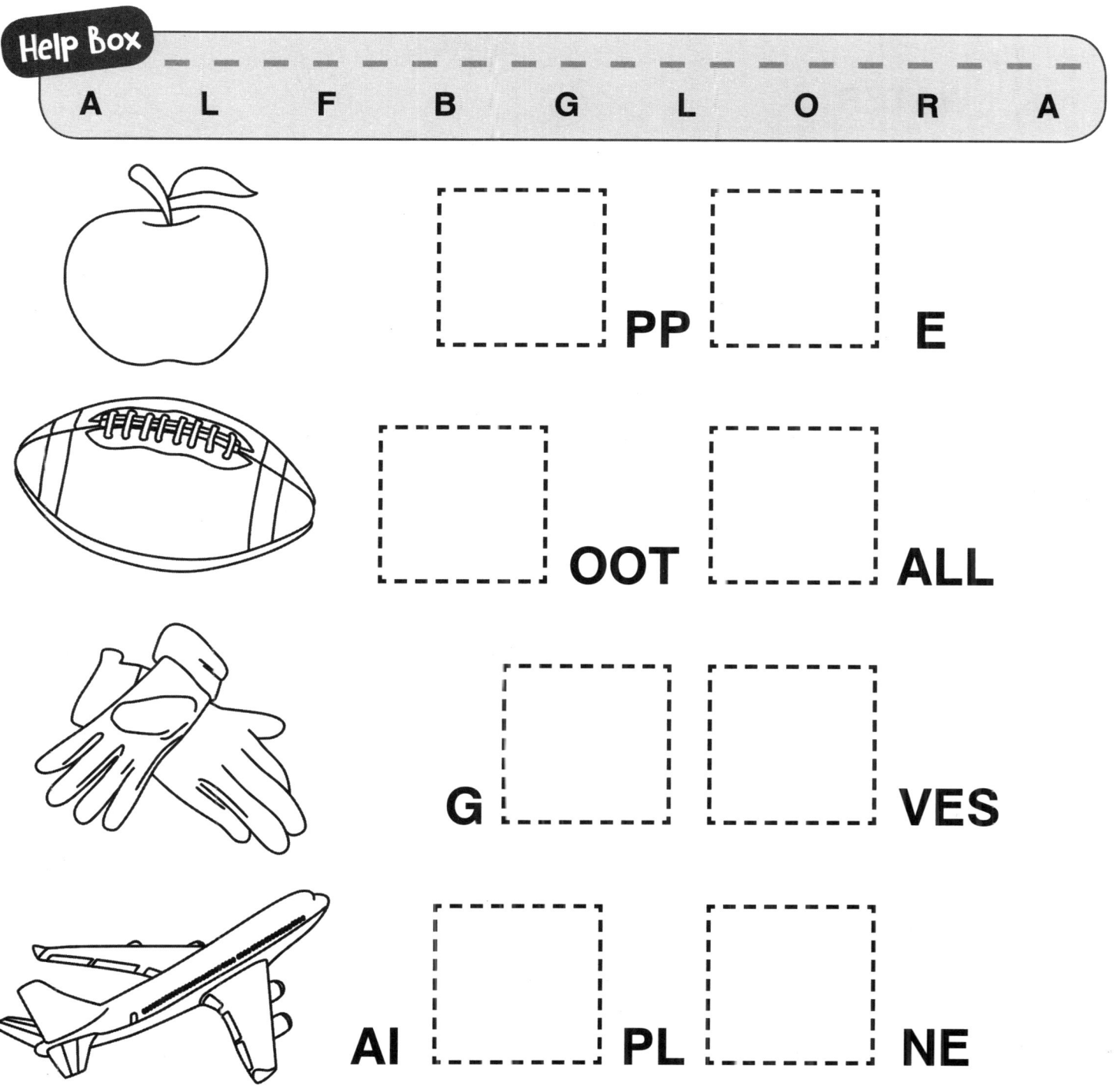

127 — I Relate To This

Fill in the missing letters. Now arrange the words in such a way that they form meaningful sentences.

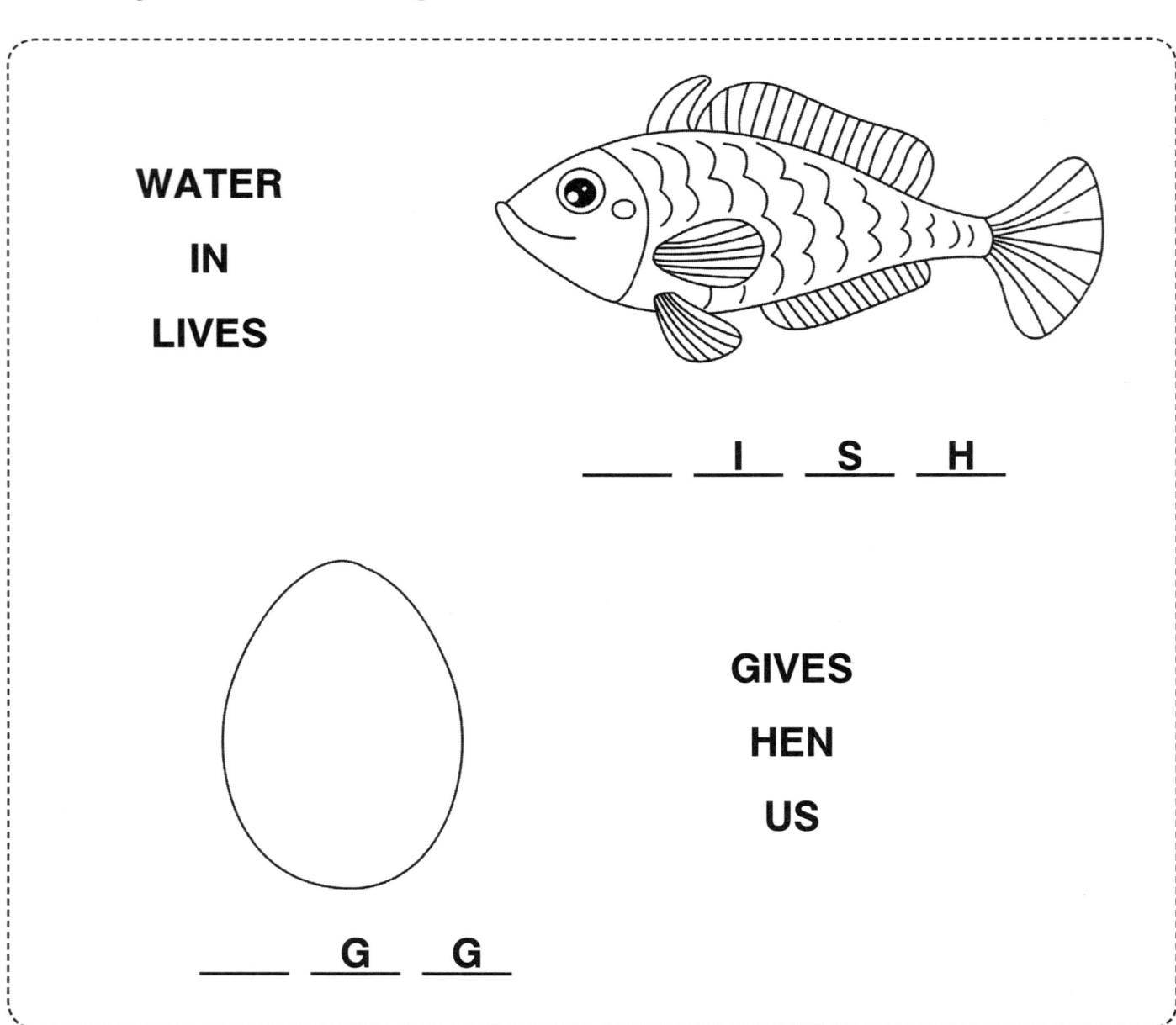

WATER
IN
LIVES

__F__ __I__ __S__ __H__

GIVES
HEN
US

__E__ __G__ __G__

Write the sentences here.

1. _____

2. _____

Date: _____   Teacher's Signature: _____

128 Spell It Out!

Identify the pictures and spell out each letter of each word loudly as you write them down.

 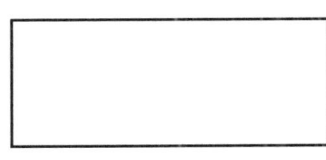    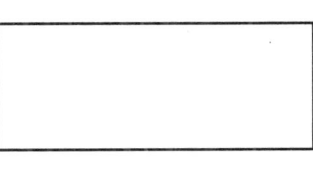

 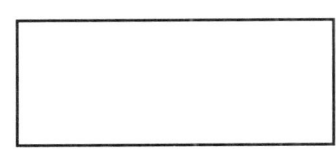

 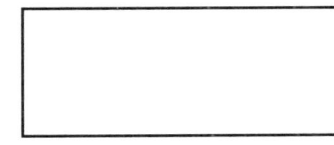

 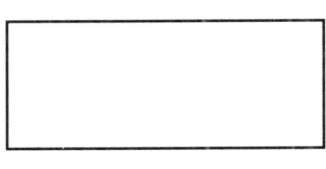    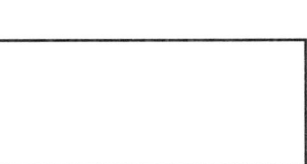

Date: _____   Teacher's Signature: _____

129 Day and Night

Circle the activities that we do in daytime and cross out the activities we do during bedtime at night.

Match Us

Match pictures that are linked to each other. One has been done for you.

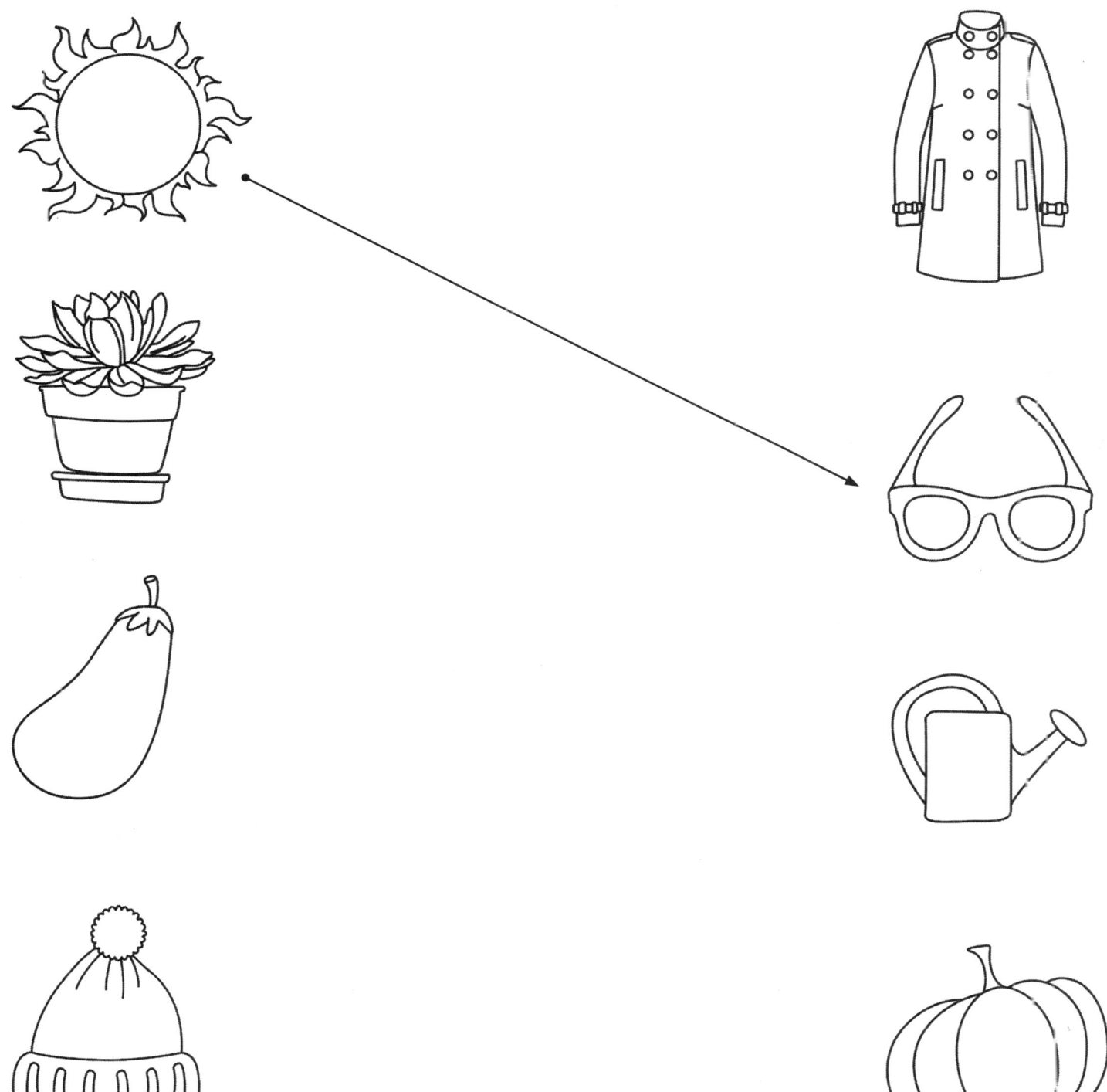

131

Word Jumble

Unscramble them and make new meaningful words.

gseg

____

lupit

____

rolwef

____

kichc

____

nubny

____

Date: __________ Teacher's Signature: _______________

Easter Puzzle

Look at the picture and clues and solve the puzzle.

Down

1. a season (6-letter word)

2. container to keep fruits, vegetables, etc. (6-letter word)

Across

2. nickname for a rabbit (5-letter word)

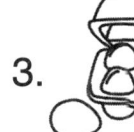
3. bird's lay them (4-letter word)

4. a festival (6-letter word)

133 The Ball is Round

Trace the sight word 'Round'.

round

round

round

A bowling ball is _____ and heavy.

Now look at the pictures carefully.

How many things in the given picture are not round? _____

Date: _____   Teacher's Signature: _____

I Feel...

Match the facial expressions with the correct word.

   Sad

   Surprised

   Frightened

135 My Workplace Tool

Draw a line to match each person with the tools they use on their job.

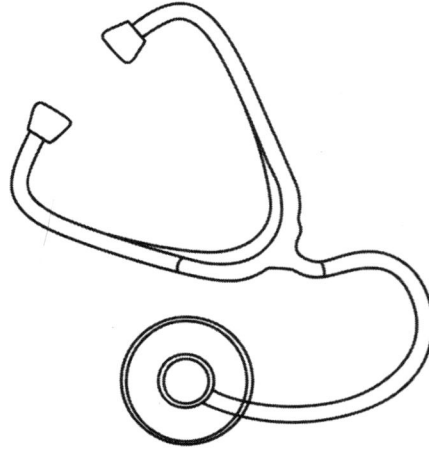

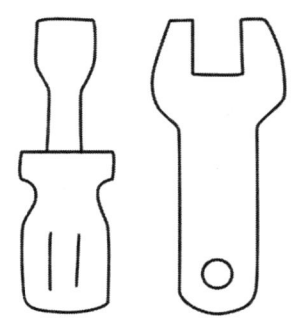

Date: _____

Teacher's Signature: _____

More Than One

Write the correct singular and plural form for each one of the following. The first one has been done for you. Get hints from the Help Box.

Help Box: scissors   bug   tree   gift

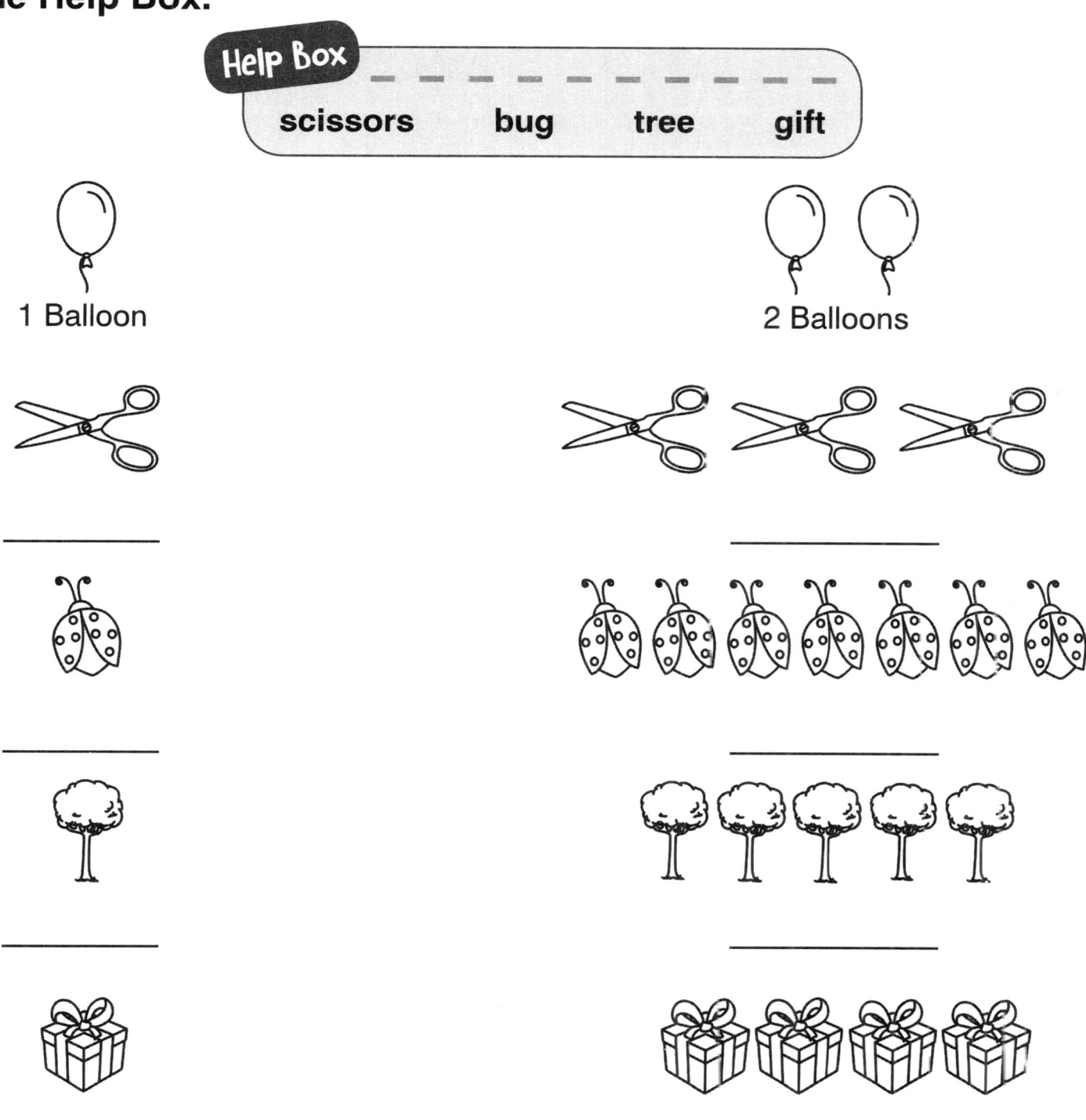

1 Balloon   2 Balloons

137 Animal Habitat

Match the animals with their homes.

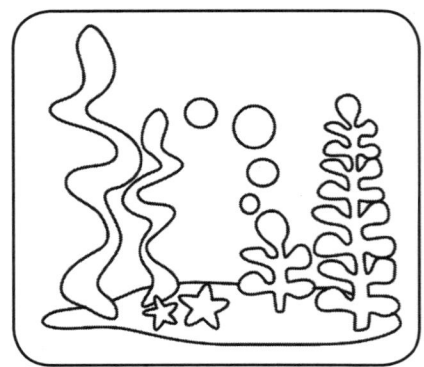

Date: _____   Teacher's Signature: _____

I Can Sense It

Match the sense organs in column A, used to sense the things in column B.

A   **B**

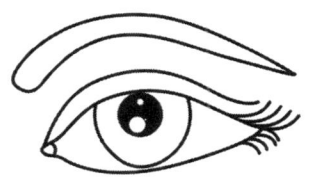   

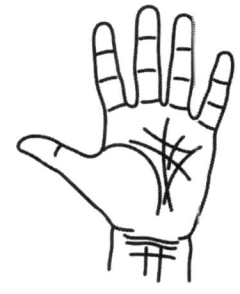   

Date: _____   Teacher's Signature: _____

139 The Weather Today Is...

Look at the two pictures. What type of day is it? Identify using words from the Help Box and write next to the pictures.

Help Box

Windy Day   Rainy day

140 Do We Sound the Same?

Match the words that sound the same.

Book

Ran

Light

Soon

Van

Write

Noon

Hook

Date: _____ Teacher's Signature: _____

141 Neither a Fruit nor a Vegetable

Circle the objects that are neither fruits nor vegetables.

How many vegetables and fruits are there in total? _____

Date: _____ Teacher's Signature: _____

142   Yes, They Are Animals

Look at the pictures given below. Circle the animals among them.

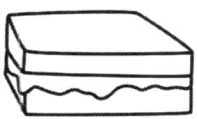  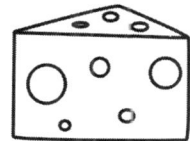 

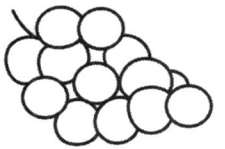   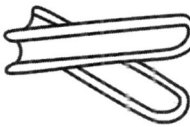

  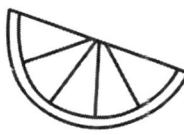 

  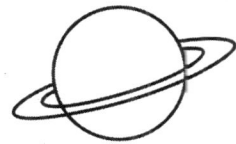 

How many animals are there? _____

Count the number of insects. _____

Date: _____   Teacher's Signature: _____

143 I Live Near

Important and easily recognisable places near your house are called landmarks. Circle a landmark that is close to your house.

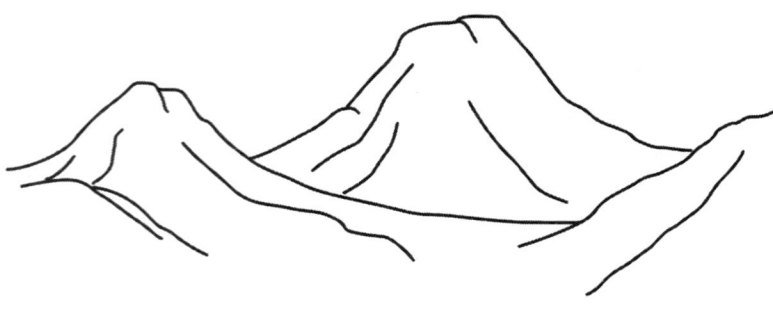
Mountains

River

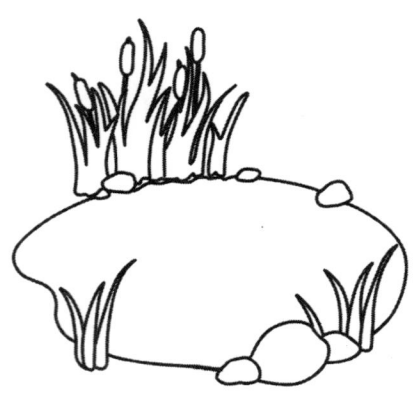
Pond

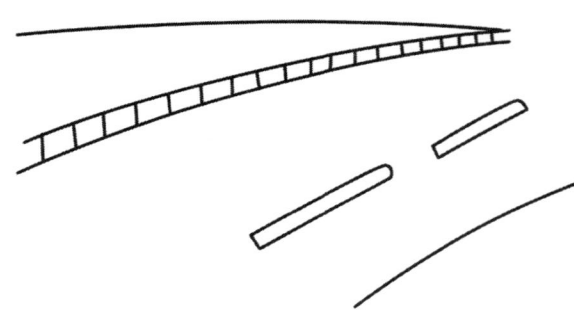
Sidewalk

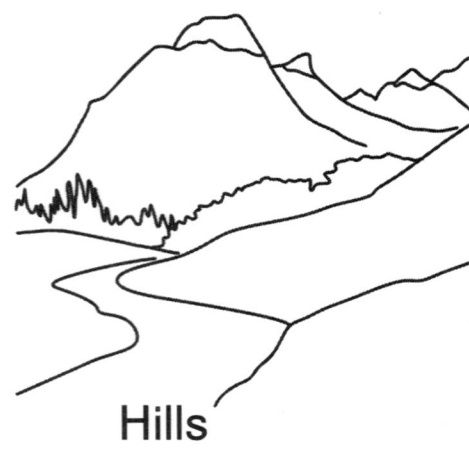
Hills

Road

Date: _____   Teacher's Signature: _____

How Many I's?

Read the rhyme loudly. Strike out each 'I' (capital and small) in the rhyme. How many are they?

The itsy-bitsy spider climbed up the water spout

Down came the rain

and washed the spider out.

Out came the sun

and dried up all the rain

and the itsy-bitsy spider climbed up the spout again.

How many I's did you find? _____

Date: _____   Teacher's Signature: _____

145 Rhyme Within a Rhyme

Count the rhyming words in the rhyme. Circle them and then write them in the blank space given below.

Hickory, dickory, dock.
The mouse ran up the clock,
the clock struck one,
the mouse ran down,
Hickory, dickory, dock.

Rhyming words: _____

Date: _____

Teacher's Signature: _____

One or Many?

Make plurals of the given words. One of them has been done for you.

flowers

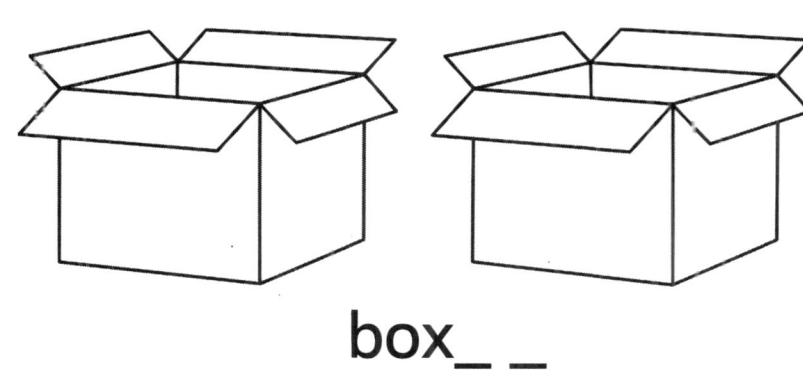
box_ _

dress_ _

bird_

tomato_ _

rabbit_

147 Animal Spelling Fun

Say the name of each animal in the pictures aloud. What is the sound that the first letter makes? Write that letter and fill in the blanks.

___onkey

___og

___lephant

___at

___ebra

'At' at the End

Say the name of each object in the pictures aloud. What is the sound that the first letter makes? Write that letter and fill in the blanks.

149 Animal First Letter

Match each picture of animal with the first letter of its name.

   F

   H

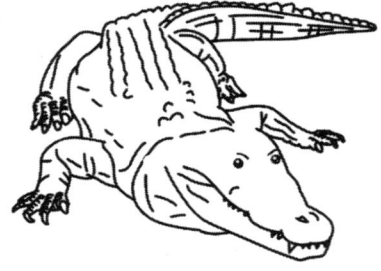   E

   C

   L

150 Same But Different

Match the words that are same but are written differently.

CAT   ball

BOY   girl

SWIM   red

RED   boy

BALL   swim

GIRL   cat

Date: _____   Teacher's Signature: _____

151   Same 'a' Sound as 'Cat'

Cat has a short 'a' sound. Read aloud the names of each picture. Circle the pictures that have the same short 'a' sound as in the word 'cat'.

Date: _____   Teacher's Signature: _____

152 Are They Rhyming Words?

Match the words that sound the same.

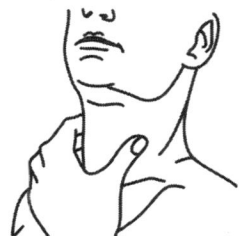
throat

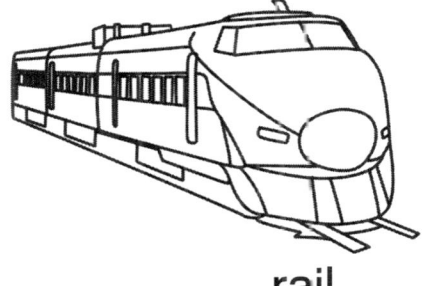
rail

son

coat

veil

pen

den

won

Reading Letters

Identify and say the name of the pictures aloud. Choose the correct beginning letter and circle it.

f r p

q i t

s m k

g t q

r b c

k s f

p n s

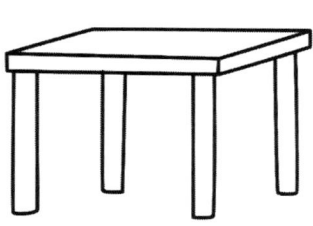

d t m

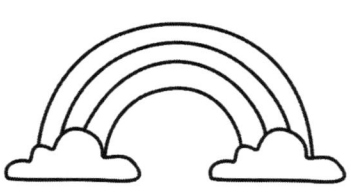

v h r

154 Picture Study

Use your imagination to fill colours into this picture. Give it a suitable title.

TITLE: _____

155 The First Letter

Identify and say the name of the pictures aloud. Choose the correct beginning letter and circle it.

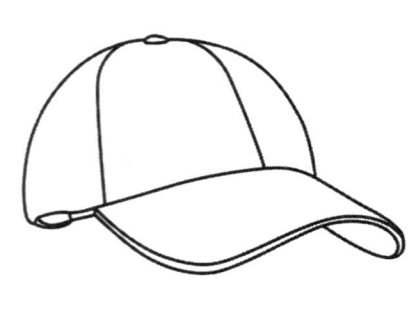

c b g

g b b

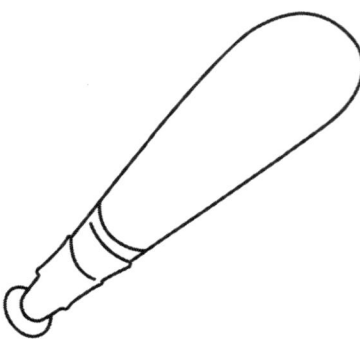

b b g

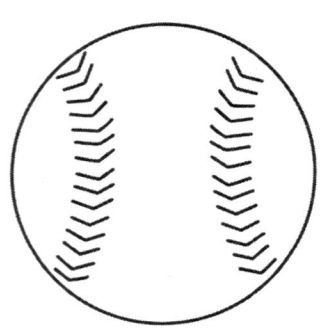

b b g

u p b

p b c

m p b

p b m

c p b

Date: _____

Teacher's Signature: _____

What Will I Wear?

These are pictures of things we will use in one of the places given in the Help Box? Circle that place and colour the things.

Help Box
Desert   Beach   Jungle

157 — Missing Letters in Haunted House!

Some letters are missing in the sequence given below. Fill the missing alphabets with small letters.

How many small letters are there? _____

How many capital letters are there? _____

Sports Time

Match the sports equipment in first column with the correct sport in the second column.

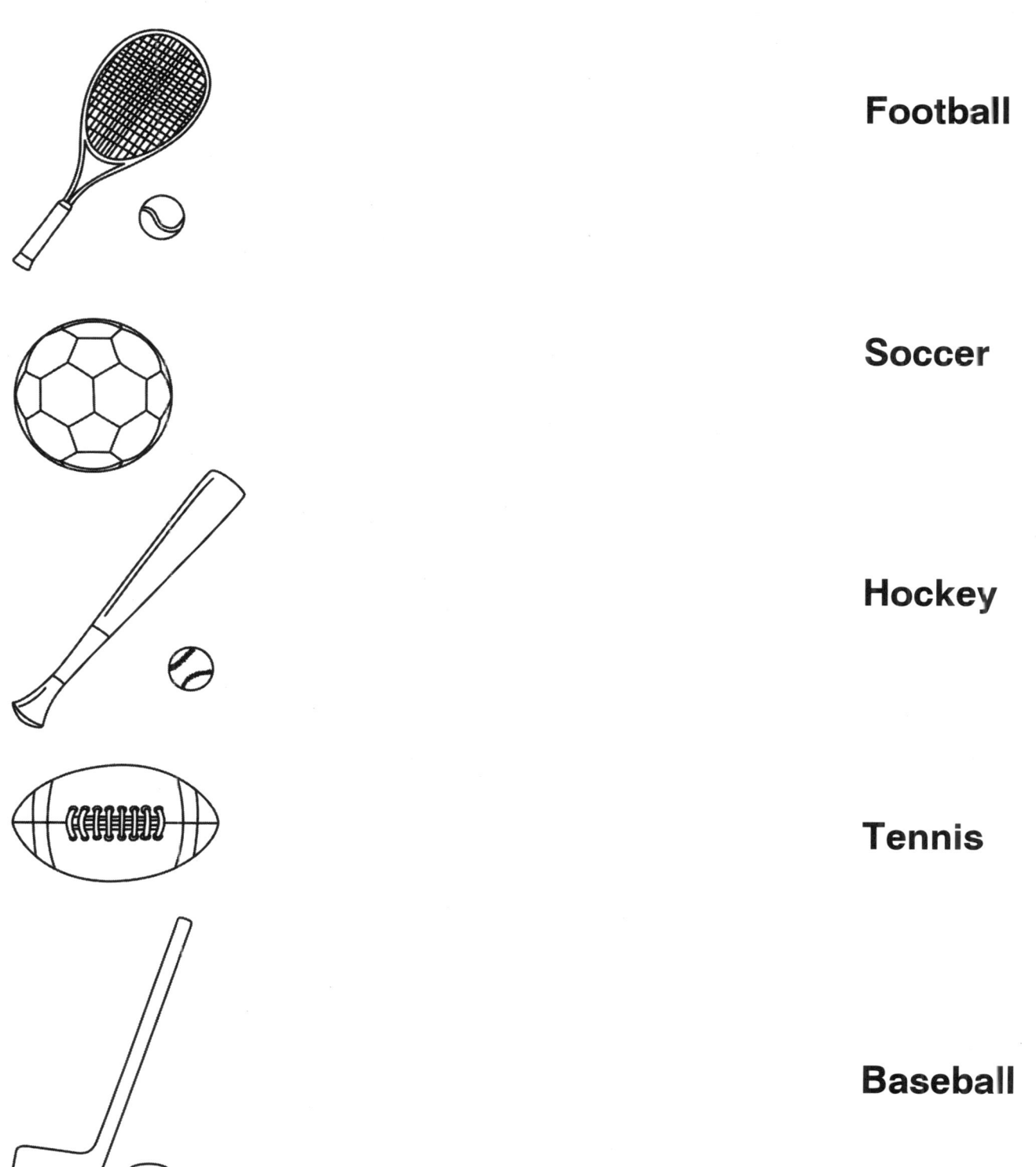

159 Who Are We?

Colour the picture given below. In which country are these animals commonly found?

160 Alphabet and Myth

Identify the alphabet and the mythical animal. Write the name of the animal below.

I am a _____ .

161   I Am a Little Teapot

Read the rhyme given below and circle the rhyming words in it.

I'm a little teapot,

short and stout.

Here is my handle.

Here is my spout.

When I get all steamed up,

hear me shout!

"Tip me over and pour me out!"

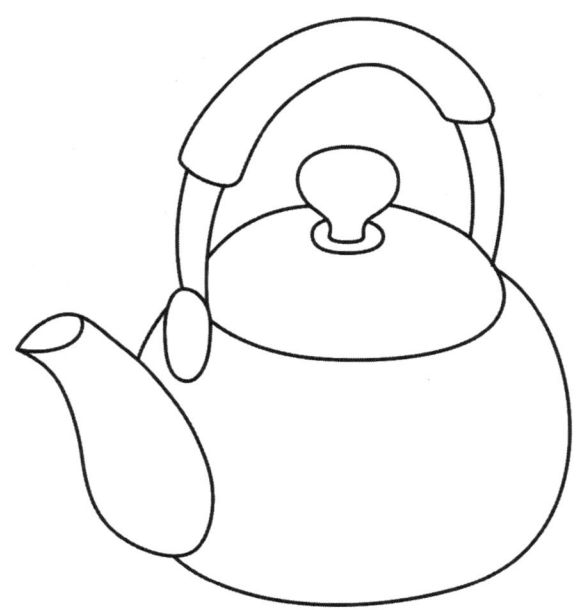

I Am a Happy Bat

Look at the picture. Why is the bat smiling? Choose one of the following reasons:

a. He just enjoyed a good meal.

b. He just met with his old friend.

c. He just enjoyed a good game with his best buddies.

d. He is going for a party.

Use your imagination to choose any one of the answers and colour the picture.

163 A Bowl of Veggies

Identify the vegetable in each bowl. Match each one with the first letter of the name.

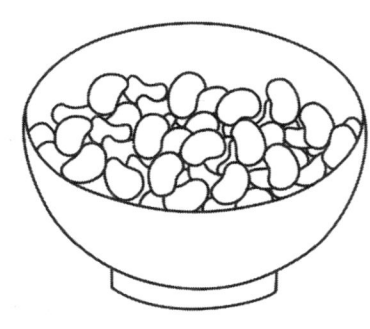

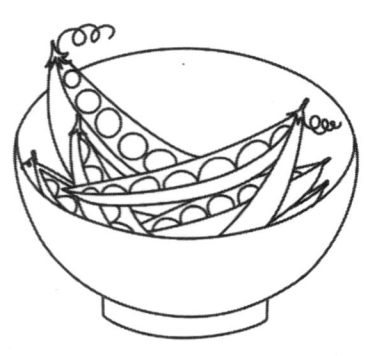

Date: _____   Teacher's Signature: _____

I Love Fruits

Identify each fruit. Then match it to the letter it begins with.

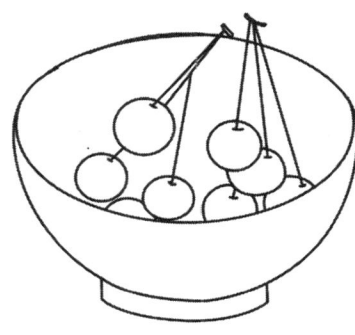 

Inside-Outside

Write 'I' under the things that belong inside the house and write 'O' under the things that belong outside the house.

Plant and Tree

Look at the pictures given below. Can you identify which one is the plant and which one is the tree?

Date: _____   Teacher's Signature: _____

167 — Different Sounds

Circle the odd one out on the basis of the sounds of their names. For example: Van-Cat-Tap. Here the odd one out is Tap.

168 | Which Game is This?

Identify the game and colour the picture.

169 The Colour Key

Use Colour Key and colour the spaces below accordingly to reveal the picture.

Colour Key

1 = Brown,   2 = Orange,   3 = Blue,   4 = Yellow,   5 = Green

How Do You Feel?

Match the facial expressions with the word that describes it.

Silly

Bored

Confused

Date: _____   Teacher's Signature: _____

171 Let's Make Up a Story

Observe the following pictures and make up a story about it.

 Pam

 Jack

 Brother-sister

 Milk

_____

_____

_____

_____

172 Off to Camp

What is the boy in the picture doing? Circle the correct option.

Help Box

Jogging   Trekking   Swimming

Date: _____   Teacher's Signature: _____

173 Family Holiday

Where is the family in the picture going? Circle the correct option.

Help Box

Jungle **Beach** **Mountains**

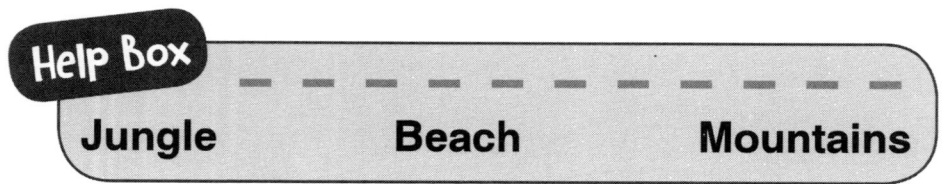

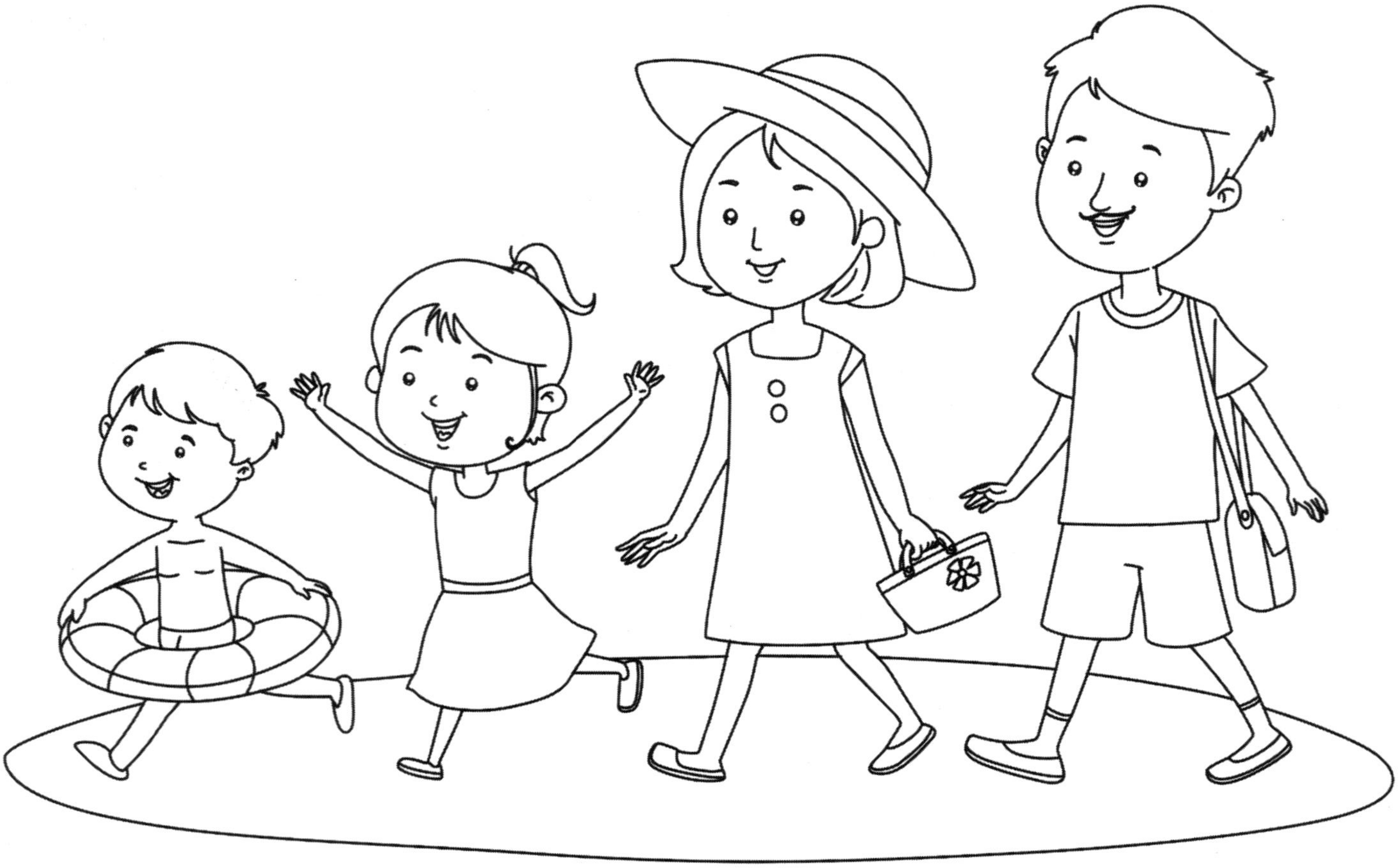

Date: ____________ Teacher's Signature: ____________

The Number Names

Search these number names from the word grid.

Help Box

Six   Seven   Eight

l	e	i	g	h	t
m	p	t	e	n	r
f	s	i	x	y	g
c	d	n	i	n	e
s	e	v	e	n	q

175 The Words With 'in'

Add the word 'in' after every letter shown in the picture and make a new meaningful word.

(Ask your parents or take help from a dictionary to find out the meaning of the words.)

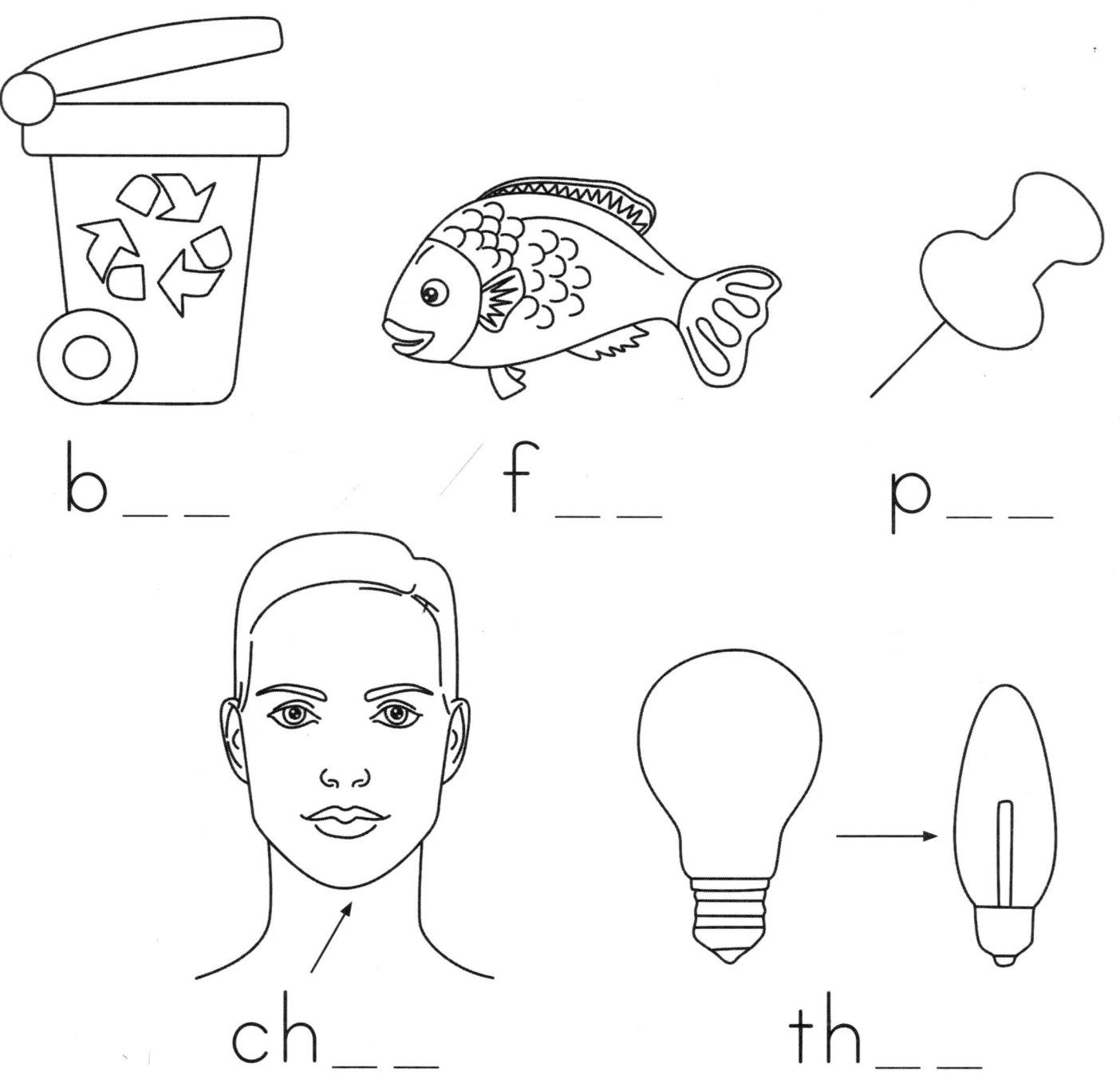

b _ _   f _ _   p _ _

ch _ _   th _ _

176 What Are We Talking About?

Imagine the scene, draw the missing object in the scene and fill in the dialogues to complete the comic strip. You can also colour it.

What is Common?

Read the names of the pictures. What do the words have in common? _____

quack

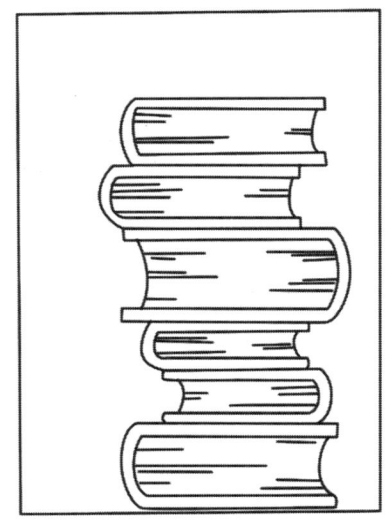
stack

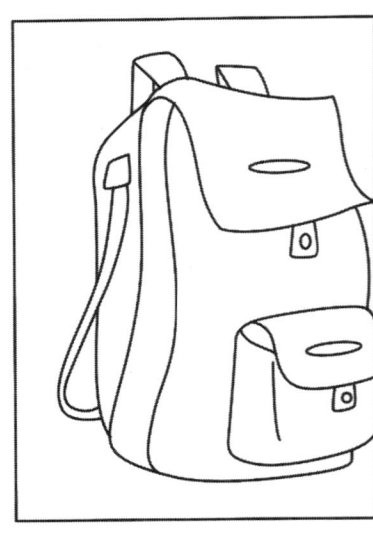
pack

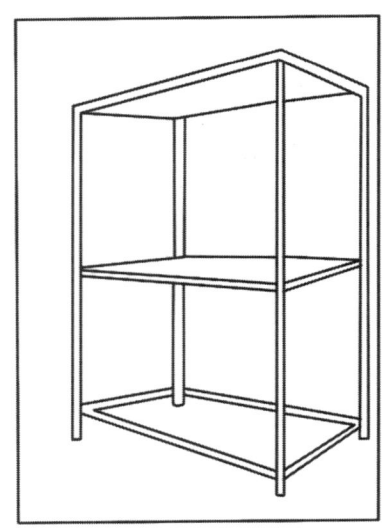
rack

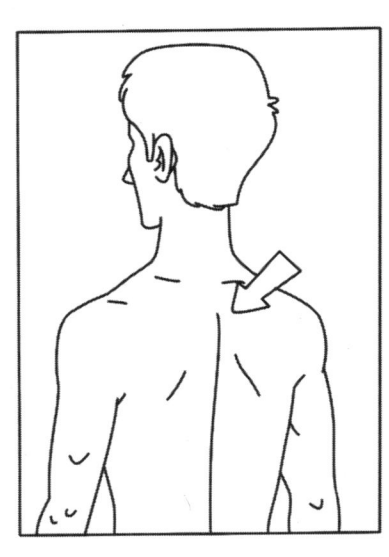
back

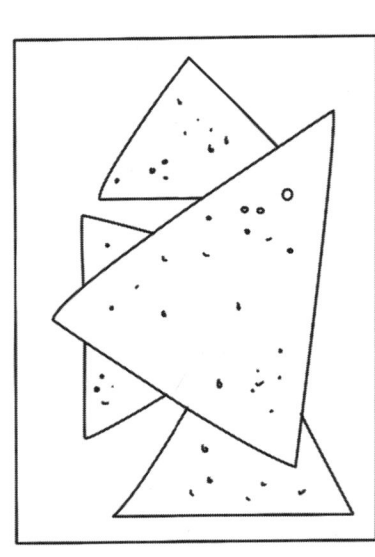
snack

178 Adding 'en'

Add 'en' at the end of each word shown in the picture and make a new meaningful word out of it.

(Ask your parents or take help from a dictionary to find out the meaning of the words.)

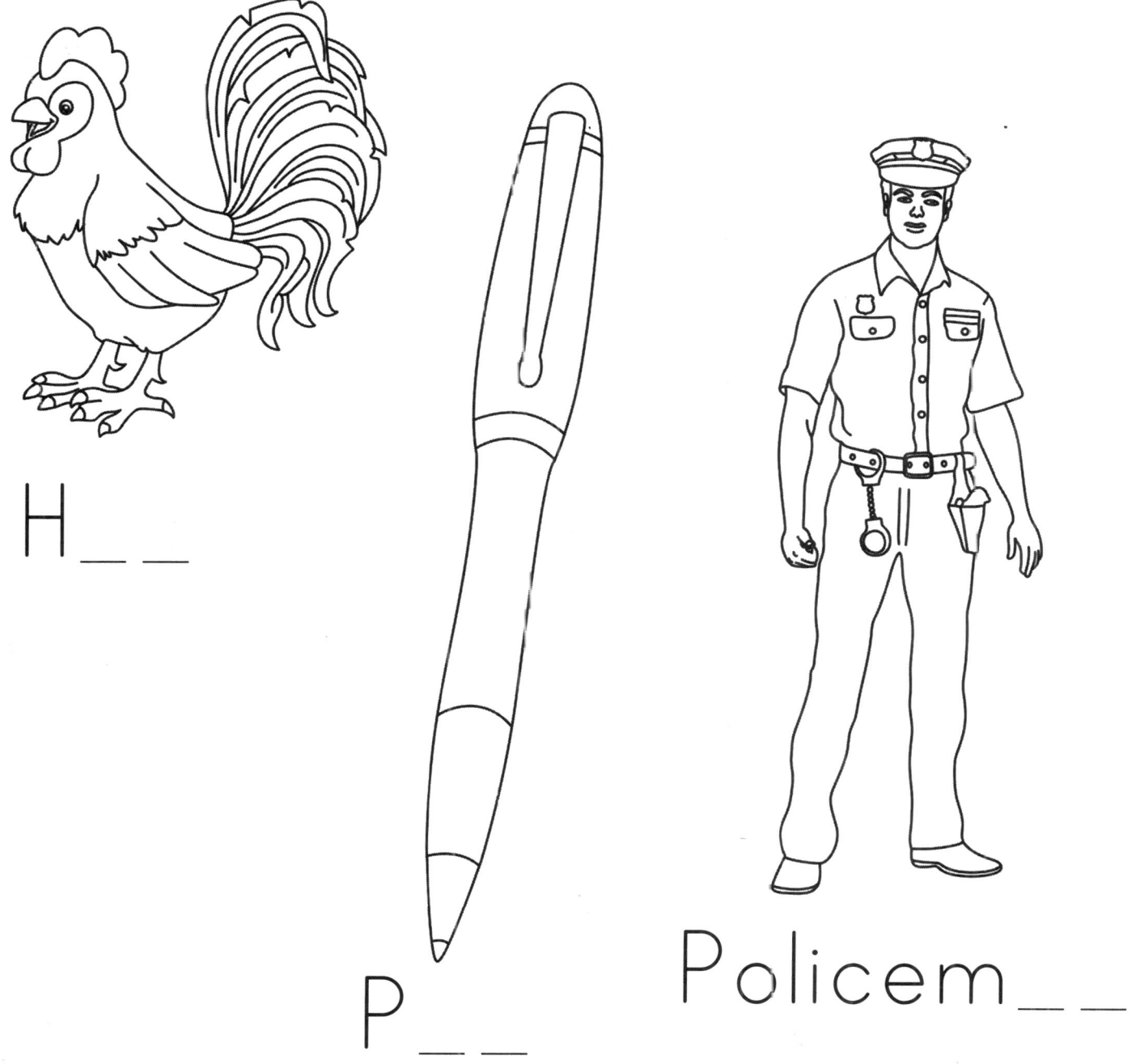

H_ _

P_ _

Policem_ _

Adding 'ig'

Add the 'ig' after every letter shown in the picture and make a new meaningful word from it.

W _ _

B _ _

D _ _

180 Colour the Airport

Have you ever been to an airport? Trace the dotted lines and colour the picture.

I Am a Bird

Choose the common letter among the words in the Help Box and complete the name of the bird.

Help Box: PIT   PAT   PAW   PEN   PAN   CUP   TAP

__ I G E O N

The Verb Search

Search and circle all the words from the Word Bank below.

Word Bank

ride   swim   walk   run   look   play   eat

R	I	D	E	L	R	X	L	H	C
X	I	H	J	D	B	E	O	I	X
A	A	X	A	I	J	G	O	O	F
S	J	X	P	V	R	S	K	E	R
W	E	N	R	J	F	F	W	L	U
I	A	Y	D	Z	S	S	A	S	N
M	T	N	P	E	M	P	L	A	Y
D	R	H	G	Y	H	T	K	S	F
M	A	B	V	L	S	I	W	N	C
Z	X	O	U	D	G	M	R	M	J

Date: _____   Teacher's Signature: _____

Let the River Flow!

183

Complete the drawing by using blue colour to trace the right path of the river from start to finish.

Date: _____ Teacher's Signature: _____

184 We Begin With

Identify and say the name of the pictures aloud. Circle the correct first letter from the choices.

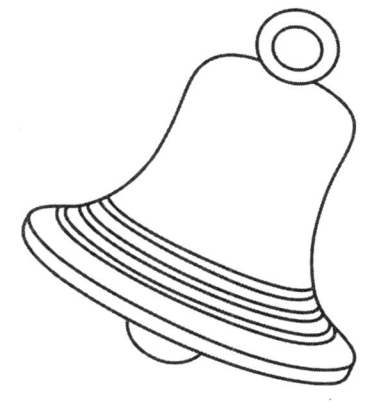

B C D

D C B

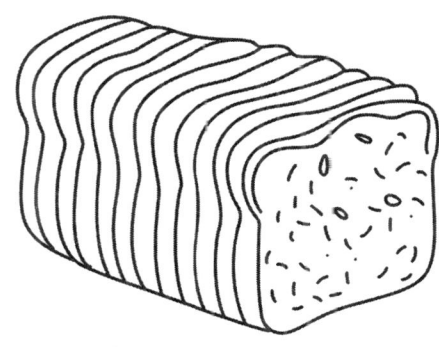

C D B

D C B

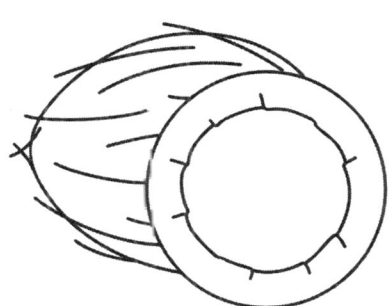

B C D

D C B

C D B

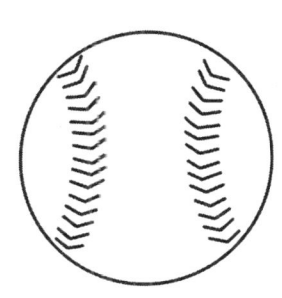

C D B

B C D

Date: _____   Teacher's Signature: _____

185 Puppy In, Puppy Out

Write 'in' when the puppy is inside the trolley and write 'out' when the puppy is outside the trolley.

 The  is _____.

 The  is _____.

The Cat Chase

Look carefully at the picture given below.

What are the animals in the picture doing?

1. Rat: _____

2. Cat: _____

Date: _____   Teacher's Signature: _____

187 Safety Slogan

Write a slogan for the picture using words from the Word Bank.

Word Bank

school	friends	ride	enjoy	play	helmet

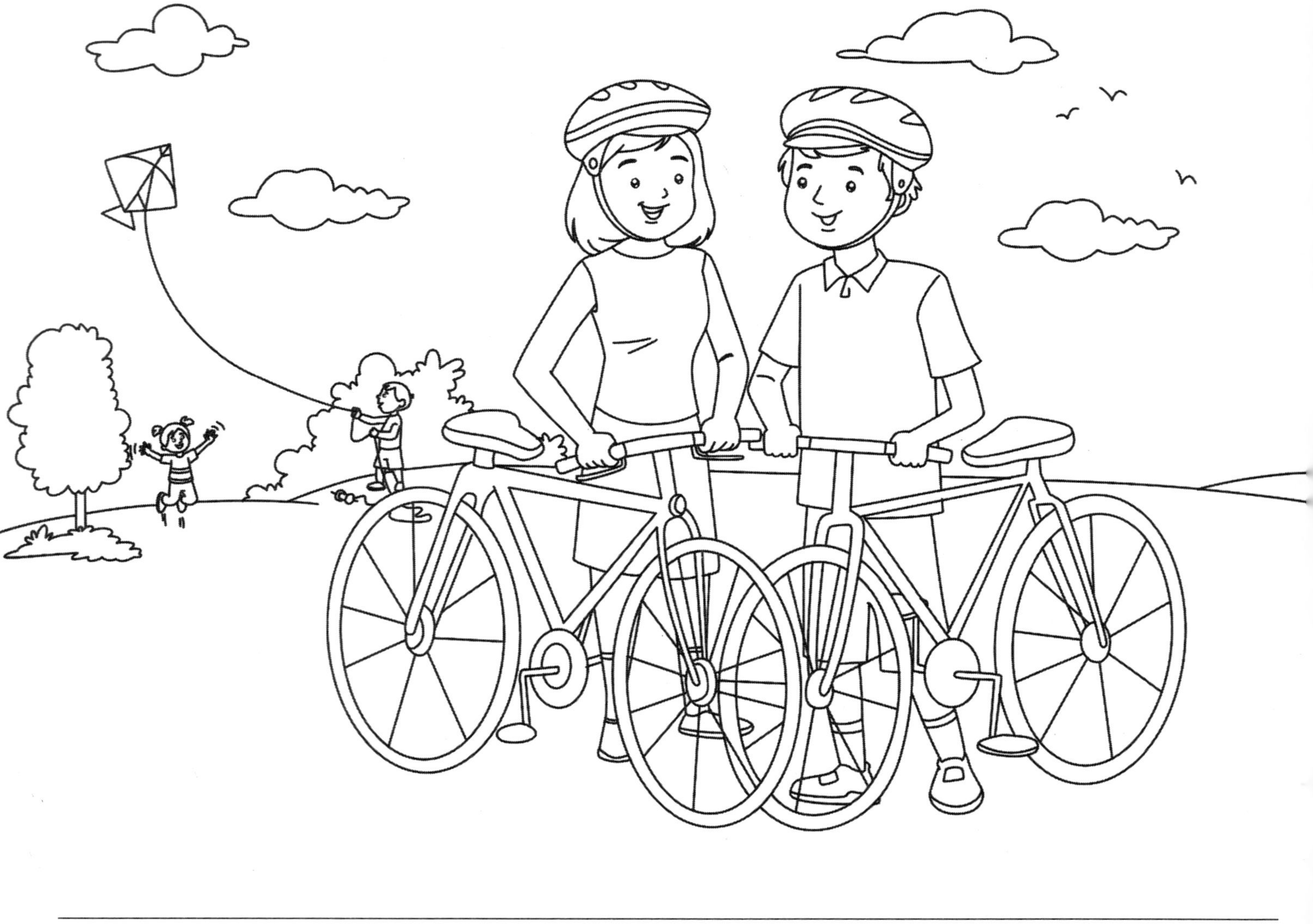

____

____

Date: ____________ Teacher's Signature: ____________

One, More than One

Read the words given below. Some of them are written in singular form and others are in plural form. Write 'S' for the singular and 'P' for plural words.

Purse _____

Wolves _____

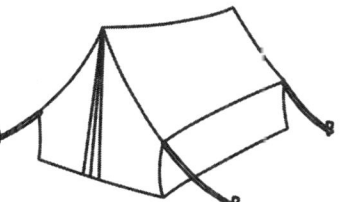

Tent _____

Candies _____

Pens _____

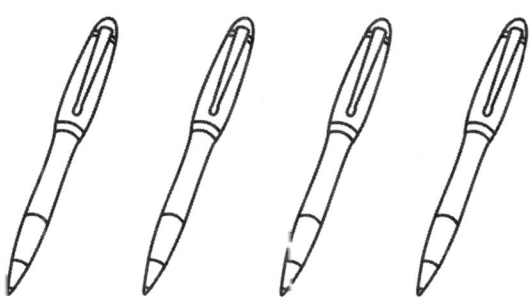

Cups _____

Date: _____   Teacher's Signature: _____

189 My Name Is Odd

Circle the picture whose name does not sound like the names of other pictures.

190 We Don't Use It Anymore

Circle the things that are used in the present and strike out those which were used in the past.

191 My Pair

Match the pictures in Column A with their pairs in Column B.

Column A   Column B

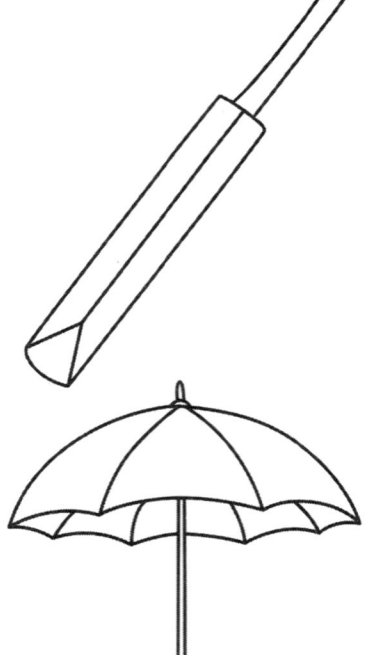   

Date: _____   Teacher's Signature: _____